PART 3 No Regrets Parenting: YOUR ADULT CHILDREN 225

PART 4 No Regrets Grandparenting 257

Acknowledgments

My deep gratitude goes to the parents and kids I've had the good fortune to work with as a pediatrician over the past forty years; they have provided me with a front-row seat from which to observe best-parenting practices. And to my colleagues—devoted pediatricians, family practitioners, psychologists, social workers, and nurses—my sincere appreciation for your role-modeling and inspiration. Thanks to Diane Debrovner at *Parents* magazine, for opening doors for me. This is the fifth book my literary agent, Lisa Leshne (The Leshne Agency), has represented for me, and I treasure our partnership and friendship; our first book together was the first edition of *No Regrets Parenting* back in 2012. I'm grateful to Samantha Jones, Jean Lucas, Kirsty Melville, and the editorial board at Andrews McMeel, for finding enough relevance in my writing to invite this second edition. Thanks also to the rest of the Andrews McMeel Publishing team for their skill and professionalism. Special thanks to my social media consultants, Emily, Samantha, and Nurit.

Finally, I am grateful to the dozens of my fellow grandparents[*] who submitted their favorite activities with their 127 grandchildren and 4 great-grandchildren for Part 4 of this book.

---

[*] Susie and Mark Barter; Jackie and Howard Bellowe; Wendy and Jim Berenbaum; Kathy and Jerry Berenstein; Krista and Mark Boscoe; Jayne and Ted Brandt; Myndie Brown and Dan Woodrow; Dina and Larry Caroline; Helayne and Jerry Cohen; Dee and Steve Daniels; Janice and Larry Fagen; Anath and Ian Gardenswartz; Erica Gardner and Larry Gray; Lea and Steve Gross; Marlane and Harvey Guttmann; Linda Heider; Dick Heider; Pia and Fred Hirsch; Adrian and Kevin Kalikow; Mari and Jack Kimel; Marcie and Phil Munishor; Eileen and John Ogle; Karen and Don Polakoff; Rachel and Nathan Rabinovitch; Laurie and Neil Segall; Bobbie and Gary Siegel; Janet and Rick Taylor; Laurie and Bill Webber; Elise Farfel Wolf and Dennis Wolf; Cindy and Mike Wolfe

Introduction—
Long Days, Short Years

he nightly news hasn't even started, but you're too exhausted to watch; who can stay awake that late?! Car pools, lunch bags, after-school activities, dinner, homework, bath time, bedtime. All on top of your own job (or jobs!) and the other realities of adulthood. You have just enough energy left to drag yourself to bed so you can wake early and start the routine all over again. Each day with young kids feels like a week, each week like a month.

But, as every new birthday passes, childhood seems to be streaking by at warp speed—five-month-olds become five-year-olds in the blink of an eye, and then fifteen-year-olds. The colorful mobiles hanging from their cribs morph into tricycles, which morph into driving permits.

And then, poof, they're gone.

Sunrise, sunset.

How can we possibly be working so hard to get through each crazy, chaotic day with our kids and yet have the years fly by so quickly? Everyone knows it, everyone bemoans it, yet no one seems to know how to slow down the years while cramming twenty-five hours into every day.

WHAT IS THIS BOOK?

I don't claim to know how to slow down time, either. But I do have some ideas about how to maximize and optimize the time you spend with your kids—while they are still tucked into their bedrooms where you can peek in on them each night before you go to sleep. This is not a book about protecting your adult priorities or nurturing your relationship

xiv NO REGRETS PARENTING

with your spouse or partner, per se. There are plenty of those books, and lots of advice out there about how to look out for your needs while still getting the kids to soccer practice on time. Rather, this is a book about how to prioritize your kids' needs within your adult schedules, and how to stretch and enhance the time you spend with your kids. And if you are able to manage those juggling acts, you'll discover something remarkable: you will be more successful in protecting adult time for yourself and your spouse or partner, and you'll feel less guilty doing it. More importantly, you'll be able to look back and take pride in knowing that you squeezed every moment and memory out of your kids' childhoods and that your kids' memories of you are vivid and loving. This is the original, one and only *No Regrets Parenting* guide, updated and expanded for today's generation of young parents. You can't do it over again, at least with these same kids, so let's do it right the first time.

And included this time around, by popular demand, are ideas for *No Regrets* Grand*parenting*. Why? Because since publication of the first edition of *No Regrets Parenting*, hundreds of grandparents have written to me (www.HarleyRotbart.com). Some have asked for advice on parenting their adult kids and in-law kids, and for those ideas, this edition of the book contains a new section called *"No Regrets Parenting Your Adult Children"* (Part 3). Other grandparents have complained about how their adult kids are raising their own kids and told me they've used the book as a "tactful" way of telling their kids to make better use of their time with their young kids; and still others have asked for help entertaining their grandkids on visits, especially when feeling less energy for playing than they had the first time around. Well, Part 4 of this book is for all of those grandparents, and the Preface to Part 4 has some suggestions for you to help your parents adjust to grandparenthood.

This is a how-to manual for time management with kids, from crib through canopy and beyond. It will help you navigate the mundane, exhausting routines of parenthood, and show you how to transform those routines into special parenting events. It's all about redefining "quality time," and that means understanding the important difference between minutes and moments.

THE FOUR CORNERS OF OUR HOUSE

With the release of the first edition of *No Regrets Parenting*, interviewers, readers of the book, and attendees at my seminars asked how the *No Regrets Parenting* concept developed. I answer by describing our house. It's a simple two-story with four bedrooms upstairs, one at each corner of the rectangle-shape footprint. My wife and I are in one corner bedroom, and the other three corners are the kids' rooms, one room per kid. But except for a few holiday weeks each year, the three kids' corner rooms are now empty—our kids have formed their own families, living their adult lives, visiting when their busy schedules allow. We walk by the kids' rooms dozens of times each day. The walls in the hallway between the bedrooms are filled with pictures of our kids at every stage of their growth and development, crib to canopy. Just like your homes, I'm sure.

Yet, as nostalgic as we are for the days when our "corners" were full and we could kiss our kids after story time and before bedtime every night, we are blessed by having *no regrets* about the amount or quality of time we spent with our kids when they were little. We were there, with them, and we made the most of the time we spent with them. We can't get the days with our young children back, but even if we could, we probably wouldn't do it any differently—which feels wonderful. That's the feeling of having *no regrets*.

WHO ARE YOU?

Before diving into *No Regrets Parenting*, you should answer one important question about yourself: Who are you?

I'm not asking who you want people to think you are, or who your parents want you to be. I'm not asking who you want to be when you grow up—as much as you may want to deny it, once you have your own kids, you are officially grown up.

Who are you? Answer honestly, because if you pretend to be someone you're not, you're going to catch up with yourself and be disappointed. To help you identify yourself, I've divided "you" into seven basic components, which I'm going to ask you to rank in order of importance. But first, here are a few definitions to use in the upcoming exercise: being a breadwinner means earning a living for yourself and your family; as a child yourself, you may see satisfying your parents' goals for you as an important priority and/or you may have increasing responsibilities for the care of your elderly parents; friend, for the purposes of this exercise, does not extend to your spouse or partner, who gets a separate category; your non-work passion qualifies you as a hobbyist—in the garden, on the tennis court or hiking trail, scrapbooking, writing poetry, playing the piano, painting; a professional is usually also a breadwinner, but many professionals see themselves and their work as more than simply earning a living; being a parent or a spouse/partner has obvious meaning.

Now, as a way of determining how you see yourself, rank those seven elements of you, with the highest priority on top, lowest priority on the bottom. I know many of you are all of these people at some time in your life, perhaps even at the same time in your life. But what is their order of importance to you?

- Breadwinner
- Child
- Friend
- Hobbyist
- Parent
- Professional
- Spouse/Partner

If in your most honest self-assessment you ranked "parent" as number one, or second only to "spouse/partner," you will find yourself at ease reading this book and you will embrace the ideas for turning scarce minutes into special moments with your kids. If, on the other hand, "parent" ranked lower than one or two on your list, *No Regrets Parenting* may initially make you feel a bit uneasy but, I hope, will motivate you to reconsider your priorities.

The intent of the advice in this book is to give you a practical and purposeful blueprint for squeezing every possible precious moment with your kids out of your hectic and harried life. If anything other than "spouse/partner" topped "parent" on the list, you are not a bad person or even an atypical person—for many, parenting is important, but not most important. But if you have other priorities that are higher than your kids, some of my suggestions may at first ring hollow—and may even feel oppressive—because they ask you to rethink how you manage other aspects of your life. If, however, you remain open to new ideas, you will find important reasons and strategies in this book to elevate the role that parenting plays in your life and leave you with *no regrets* when walking past their empty bedrooms someday.

You may argue that being a professional first and/or making a good living as breadwinner makes you a better parent. And that may well be true. But the goal of *No Regrets Parenting* is not just to make you a better parent. It's to make you a parent who is there, with your kids, from crib to canopy, without neglecting your other responsibilities. Nostalgia is normal and good; it means your kids' childhoods were loving and meaningful for you. But there should be *no regrets*.

Okay, that's not entirely fair. When looking back someday, everyone will have some regrets about their parenting experiences. Perhaps you may wish you had taught your kids more about literature and art, encouraged more reading, or perhaps you will regret not helping your kids learn to budget or save or invest. You might wish you had sent your kids to different schools or taken them to church more often. But here's the real meaning of *No Regrets Parenting*—we should never regret not spending enough time with our kids or not getting to really know them. I've written this book in hopes of helping you make the most of your time with your kids, no matter how busy you are and no matter how many conflicting priorities you have. Moreover, this book will also help you actually create more time with your kids than you ever thought you could.

So if parenting is at the top of your life priorities list, what about your spouse or partner? Shouldn't they be the top priority in your life? How many sad stories have you heard of couples struggling in their relationship because their kids, careers, and other commitments are all-consuming? Yes, I hope your spouse or partner is also number one or two on your priority list. Any lower than that and you need a different resource to help work out those issues. *No Regrets Parenting* assumes that you and your partner are in sync in your relationship and in your goals to maximize the time you have with your kids. Unfortunately, that's not always the case. As I speak around the country about *No Regrets Parenting*, countless parents asked this question from the audience or afterward in private—What should I do if my husband/wife/partner doesn't feel as strongly about parenting as I do? If you're on different pages about the meaning and magic of parenting, I hope reading this book together will help you harmonize your priorities and realize that being an intimate and integral part of your kids' lives gives you new opportunities to strengthen your bond to each other, as well. I would be thrilled to take credit for bringing you and your partner even closer together.

Know yourself, and stay true to yourself. This book is for those of you who shudder at the thought of your kids growing up too fast, leaving for college, career, or canopy, becoming young adults. Of course you want growth and independence for your kids, but only after you've squeezed every drop of joy and wonder from their childhoods. *No Regrets Parenting* arms you with the tools you need to meet those eventualities with contentment and fulfillment: contentment that comes with knowing you were there, with your kids, every moment you could have been; and fulfillment that comes with knowing you created new, cherished moments that otherwise might have been lost in the quest for expediency. In fact, if you learn and apply the basics of *No Regrets Parenting*, you will greet your children's departure with a profound sense of satisfaction, knowing you have given them what they need to succeed and given yourself what you need to feel like a successful parent. A *no regrets* parent. To be sure, you'll gaze into their empty bedrooms and miss them terribly when they leave home. But you won't have missed them when they were still at home.

The days are long, but the years are short. And now is the time.

HOW TO READ THIS BOOK

I may be unique as an author in suggesting that the bathroom can be an ideal spot to keep this little volume. The book is not written to be read cover to cover. In fact, what parent with young kids has the time, or the concentration, to read anything cover to cover? And since this book is all about time management and finding balance, each chapter is short and written to stand on its own. So, pick and choose, skip around. How much you read in a single sitting really depends on how long you need to be sitting . . . if you catch my meaning.

Alternatively, tuck the book into the glove box of your car and pull it out for a quick fix while you're in line at the drive-through or waiting in the school pickup zone. Or perch it on your nightstand for a little inspirational reading before sleep—although there is a clear risk that the book will get you so worked up about great new plans with your kids for tomorrow that you won't be able to fall asleep!

Part 1 of this book lays out the basic principles, and Part 2 provides specific strategies in the practice of *No Regrets Parenting*. Each part is important, but you should probably read the first part first. That's why it's the first part. And be aware, there may be chapters in Parts 1 and 2 where you say to yourself, "Of course, that's OBVIOUS!" Or, "That's so OLD-FASHIONED!" First, what's obvious or old-fashioned for you won't be the same as for others. But, even more importantly, the "obvious" and "old-fashioned" tend to be taken for granted and overlooked, so read those chapters as a reminder that obvious and old-fashioned ideas have been time-tested and proven for countless generations of parents and children. They work.

Part 3 then launches you into the exciting (terrifying?) world of parenting adult kids, while Part 4 braces you for the new challenges of your kids having kids. So, pass this book along to your own parents who should start with Part 4, "*No Regrets* Grand*parenting.*" Then they can work their way back for great activity ideas with their grandkids. Whereas the first edition of this book often found its way from grandparents to their adult kids, hoping to nudge them toward better parenting time management, with this second edition, the flow of the book can go in both directions.

THE PANDEMIC "ELEPHANT IN THE ROOM"

As I'm writing this second edition of *No Regrets Parenting*, the devastating COVID-19 pandemic is showing early signs of coming under control. Vaccines and new, more successful treatments are being deployed. My specialty within pediatrics is infectious diseases, and my research for more than forty years has focused on viral infections in children and adults. Needless to say, I have been consumed with interest and inquiries regarding the pandemic, and I've given much thought to how the pandemic should be addressed in this new edition of *No Regrets Parenting*. But as I carefully updated and expanded this book, I was gratified to realize that the advice I give for *No Regrets Parenting* is independent of the pandemic—the basic principles and strategies for making the most of the precious minutes with your young children (and grandchildren), turning those minutes into meaningful moments, are as important during a pandemic as before and after a pandemic. *No Regrets Parenting* doesn't change because of a virus—if anything, it becomes even more important. So, this will be my only mention of the pandemic, but know that it was on my mind with every sentence I wrote, and I hope you'll agree that the relevance of the *No Regrets Parenting* approach and philosophy is timeless.

STAY IN TOUCH

Email me with your own suggestions and brainstorms—I'll work as many of your ideas into my *No Regrets Parenting* blog as possible. Find my email contact, as well as the blog, at www.HarleyRotbart.com. One such note I received, my favorite so far, is reprinted in the Epilogue of this book.

PART 1

No Regrets Parenting
Basic Principles

The Checkered History
of Parenting Advice

*L*ooking back at the evolution of parenting advice over the centuries, it seems to me that Adam and Eve may have been the only parents in history without the benefit of an "advice du jour book" on how to raise children. Admittedly, considering how things worked out for their kids, our original forebears probably could have used a book or two on the subject. But surely if Adam and Eve would have had two parenting books on their shelf in the garden, each book would have advocated a diametrically different parenting philosophy.

Seventeenth-century poet and nobleman John Walmot is famously quoted as saying, "Before I got married I had six theories about bringing up children; now I have six children and no theories." Parenting experts—from psychologists and pediatricians to philosophers, clergy, kings, queens, and First Ladies—have all opined in learned and not-so-learned treatises and bestselling books on how best to raise kids. Slow parenting, helicopter parenting (now drone parenting!), free-range parenting, and attachment parenting. Soccer moms and stay-at-home dads. Nurturant parenting, positive parenting, strict parenting, ethical parenting, indulgent parenting, authoritative parenting, and authoritarian parenting. Or you can take a stroll through the literary parenting "zoo": dolphin parenting, panda parenting, elephant parenting, and jellyfish parenting. Really! Then there are the international flavors: French parenting, Danish parenting, Dutch parenting, and don't forget the Chinese "Tiger Moms." Spanking, praising, scolding, rewarding, tough love, and safety-net love. Another day, another dollar spent on another expert's theory.

Okay, so I know you're thinking: Isn't this a parenting book you're reading? No, not in the traditional sense of books giving advice on parenting styles and philosophies. This is a time management book for parents—and grandparents—to make the most of their time with their children and grandchildren.

So, what is the best parenting philosophy you should use to raise your children? Forgive me, but I'm going to duck that question. Over the past forty years as a pediatrician, when it seemed appropriate, I have given parenting advice to young parents and not-so-young parents, using my doctor's intuition to judge the individual circumstances and choose the best parenting approach to suggest. At home with our own three kids, my wife and I have relied on our parenting intuition, probably crisscrossing through a hodgepodge of experts' recommendations without even knowing it. And in the end, I have concluded that there is no single "right" way to raise kids. The unique circumstances and dynamics in your household will guide you in developing your own parenting intuition, or they may even guide you toward a book from a particular parenting guru whose advice best fits your family. There is, however, a single truth that applies to any parenting philosophy you may choose: Your kids need you to be there. They need to see who you are and how you live your life. And in return, they will help you to *better* see who you are and how you *should* live your life.

So, now for a question that I won't duck: How can you be there for your kids in the way they need you and in the way you need them? The simple answer: find enough time. Regardless of the approach to parenting you choose, the moments you have with your kids are fleeting and precious. This book doesn't deal much with particular parenting philosophies. This is a book about time—finding enough of it and making the most of it.

940 Saturdays and the "Other" Biological Clock

Remember holding your new baby during those first moments in the delivery room? You shed tears of gratitude for the miracle in your arms and felt the joy and relief of knowing the waiting for pregnancy and childbirth was over. But, ready or not, in those first moments you also started the timer on the "other biological clock" facing young parents—you're now ticking down the fleeting moments of childhood.

The most enduring notion from the first edition of this book, spawning its own book and thousands of articles and blog posts, is this: There are only 940 Saturdays between those magical moments in the delivery room and the momentous day your little miracle graduates from high school, moving on to her young adult life—college, career, canopy. GRADUATES FROM HIGH SCHOOL!!!

When you add up all the time your kids spend at day care, in school, asleep, at friends' homes, with babysitters, at camp, and otherwise occupied with activities that don't include you, the remaining moments in their days become especially precious. Though 940 Saturdays may sound like a lot, how many have you already used up? If your child is five years old, 260 Saturdays are gone. Poof! How did you spend them? And the older your kids get, the busier their Saturdays get with friends and activities. Ditto Sundays.

And what about weekdays? Are you kidding?! Depending on your child's age, there may be as few as one or two hours a day during the week for you to spend with him. When kids are very young, they sleep through many of your hours together. When they're a little older, school, homework, your work schedule, and their playdates turn Mondays into Fridays with little time to catch your breath or catch up with your kids.

Once the miracle of childbirth occurs, every day brings new growth, new milestones, and new wonderment. But the challenges of juggling our adult lives often prevent us from fully appreciating the delicate nuances of childhood.

Yet the biological clock of parenthood continues to tick. Of course, there are also 940 Tuesdays and 940 Fridays, and even though those days are busier than weekends, you've still got plenty of time, so don't panic. *No Regrets Parenting* just asks that you rethink your parenting— how are you spending the time you have with your young kids? Are they watching TV while you're doing the laundry or preparing dinner? Are they playing video games while you're catching up on email? Do you take them in the car on your errands with a DVD or their cell phones performing hypnosis in the backseat? Do you resent the distractions from your daily routine that the kids cause? If you answered "yes" to any of those questions, it's time to readjust your inner clock: stop counting "minutes spent" with your kids and start accumulating "moments shared." Don't measure the time you allow yourself to spend with your kids each day, but rather ask yourself how you made that time memorable. The strategies in Part 2 of this book will help you take scarce minutes and turn them into special moments—precious moments that, in the aggregate, will leave you fulfilled and satisfied when your kids are grown.

Here's a mental trick to help you readjust your thinking from minutes to moments. In the course of each bedtime's bedlam, try to see into the future. The next time the clamor crescendos, but before the din dims, imagine your biological parenthood clock wound forward to the time when they're grown and have left home. Picture their formerly tousled bedrooms as neat, clean, and empty. See the tidy backseat of the car, vacuumed and without crumbs or Cheerios. Playroom shelves neatly stacked with dusty toys. Laundry under control. Then wind the imaginary clock back from the future to now, and see these minutes of mayhem for what they are, finite and fleeting moments. Never to be reproduced. Precious.

The Developmental
Milestones of Parenthood

"The value of marriage is not that adults produce children, but that children produce adults."
—Peter De Vries, American novelist and humorist (1910–1990)

C hildhood developmental milestones captivate parents, grandparents, doctors, and psychologists. When a baby first rolls from front to back, first sits, first walks, utters her first words, and countless other benchmarks leading up to graduation from high school and leaving home for college or career. Volumes have been written to guide observers in tracking kids' developmental progress. But often lost in the glow of babies' accomplishments are the parallel milestones parents achieve after their kids are born.

Parenthood is, arguably, the most unique period in an adult's life. Experts studying the changes that take place in new parents find that many of them are truly transformative, fundamentally changing the way adults think and act. You certainly have recognized some of those changes in yourself as you became a parent, and they go far beyond the obvious ones of mastering the bandaging of boo-boos or changing diapers without gagging.

As with childhood developmental milestones, parental growth is not a step ladder, but a gradual and phased ramp of growth. However, much as the age of a child's first steps and first words can be roughly predicted, I believe there are reliable markers you can anticipate along your developmental path as a parent. So, herein are Rotbart's Developmental Milestones of Parenting. These are based on your evolution as a parent with your first child because by the time the second one arrives, you have already reached and gone beyond these phases of parental maturity, or maybe by then you're just too tired to notice.

MILESTONE 1. THE WOMB—NURTURING, NESTING, AND NAUSEA

The parenting adventure hasn't even started yet, but there are great expectations mixed with apprehension and mystery. How is it possible that each edition of books for expectant parents gets thicker and more intense than the previous edition? How can there be so much to learn and prepare? What did expectant parents do before books?

MILESTONE 2. BIRTH TO 1 MONTH—FEAR, SHOCK, AND AWE

Everything about your first newborn is, well, new! You don't even begin to know how much you don't know, but you're sure there's a lot. How did your parents ever do this? How did the neighbors? Add to that sense of ignorance a creeping sense of panic, and a sense of responsibility like nothing you've ever felt before—not with a new car, a new house, or a new job. NOTHING puts more weight on your shoulders than a seven-pound baby.

MILESTONE 3. ONE MONTH TO 3 MONTHS—WARMTH AND WIDE-EYED WONDER

Now we're finally getting somewhere! Eye contact, babbling, and smiling all reassure you that there may be a little person hidden in this bundle of blankets and diapers. Colic reminds you the emerging little person may be gassy. This is the developmental phase of parenting when intense bonding takes place because the interactions with your baby are now more consistently two-way, and if she's smiling, you must be doing something right.

MILESTONE 4. THREE MONTHS TO 7 MONTHS —VAUDEVILLE AND VARIETY SHOWS

Parents now go through what appears to the rest of the world to be a developmental regression: talking baby talk, making goofy noises and silly faces, daffy dancing, silly singing, and perpetual peek-a-boo'ing. Whatever it takes for your baby to give you one of those belly laughs that turn your insides to goo.

MILESTONE 5. SEVEN MONTHS TO 12 MONTHS —BIOGRAPHER AND CURATOR

Although your baby's first smile and first laugh are unforgettable events of earlier stages of parenthood, now the "firsts" come fast and furiously. The first time your baby sits, pulls to a stand, takes steps, utters a word. These are the firsts you'll remember most, the ones you'll write down and film for posterity. More photographs are taken per minute during this phase of parenting than any other. This is also the phase of parenthood when you start worrying about keeping up with the Jones baby's milestones. Why is that other baby in mom-tot class already sitting without support? Is she more advanced than my baby? How will I ever get my little girl into a good preschool if she can't sit without support? Without a good preschool education, will she ever get into a good college?

MILESTONE 6. ONE YEAR TO 2 YEARS—SECRET SERVICE AGENT (STAGE 1)

Parents are now in full bodyguard and gatekeeper mode from the time your toddler wakes up until the time he's asleep for the night (if you're so lucky). Your baby's mobility and curiosity are soaring, and the dangers surrounding him become your constant obsession. There are so many ways to get hurt, you're feeling like you always have to be one step ahead of your little adventurer. And, I'm afraid, you're right.

THE DEVELOPMENTAL MILESTONES OF PARENTHOOD **11**

MILESTONE 7. TWO YEARS TO 3 YEARS—BAD GUY (STAGE 1)

This is when parents teach boundaries and rules to their kids, and, in doing so, learn to live with being the "bad guy." Parents of toddlers say "no" more than any other word, which is excellent practice for having teenagers (when you enter Bad Guy Stage 2). Although experts extol the virtues of limit-setting and structure for kids, that doesn't help with the guilt you're feeling as the constant naysayer. Adding to the household negativity, your toddler has also learned to say "no," and says it often.

MILESTONE 8. THREE YEARS TO 5 YEARS—BEST FRIENDS FOREVER

How early are your own first childhood memories? Most adults can recall certain events from when they were 3 or 4 years old. This is the age when your kids are beginning to form their lifelong memories, and just in time because they are now developmentally able to do so many more memorable activities than before; your child is now a tricycler, climber, artist, and actor. And now is when all the questions start— Whyyyy, Mommy? Howwww, Daddy? Better get your answers ready, because this is the parenting stage when you should become your kids' best friend forever. This is when they learn to come to you not only with constant questions but with their "exaggerated" problems. Although you see them as exaggerated, to your kids their problems are the most important thing in their lives—at least for the next five minutes. School hasn't started yet, so you are still their primary source of wisdom and comfort. If you handle this right, they'll keep sharing their issues with you when they're older and their problems are bigger, even though by then they'll have others competing to answer their questions and sympathize with their crises. But those other best friends aren't as caring and devoted as you are, and now is the stage to earn your kids' trust for the future.

MILESTONE 9. FIVE YEARS TO 7 YEARS—LETTING GO (STAGE 1)

Some parents are jubilant about their child's first day of kindergarten (see the upcoming chapter "The Independence Days of Childhood"); others, not so much. In describing grief, Elizabeth Kübler-Ross noted five distinct stages: denial, anger, bargaining, depression, and acceptance. Just sayin' . . .

MILESTONE 10. SEVEN YEARS TO 10 YEARS—CHAUFFEUR, CHOREOGRAPHER, AND CRUISE DIRECTOR

Your kids' calendar is now filled up, and the tires on your car are worn down. Juggling their schedules with your work and/or other commitments could be a full-time job for someone trained as a party planner or White House Chief of Staff. But since you can't afford to hire either, this is when you realize your kids are busier than you, and you must master parental organization.

MILESTONE 11. TEN YEARS TO 12 YEARS—TWEENER AND LIFE COACH . . . AND SECRET SERVICE AGENT (STAGE 2)

The so-called "tween" years of your kids' lives are also tween years in yours. You are now transitioning from a period of reasonable control over your kids' lives (seven to ten years) to the next phase (twelve to fifteen years) when you lack all sense of control over anything. Your crisis management and stress management skills will be tested in a gentler and kinder way than they will be a few years from now, so this is the time to establish healthy parental coping patterns in preparation for what's to come. This is also when you become your kids' life coach—anticipating the challenges they will have as teens, you may now feel an uncontrollable urge to tell them everything they'll ever need to know in their whole lives. That's okay, but periodically check to see they're still listening or if they've put their earbuds back in.

And speaking of earbuds, this is the age group that frequently first joins social media. The risks to health and safety in the cyberworld are as great or greater than those when the kids were stumbling into table corners as toddlers. And protecting your kids from cyber risks is much more difficult than putting pads on the table corners (see "Social Media" in Part 2).

MILESTONE 12. TWELVE YEARS TO 15 YEARS—BAD GUY (STAGE 2)

This is when you catch yourself sounding like your own parents, something you promised you'd never do. The word "no" returns to your vocabulary with a vengeance. The early teen years force you to answer the question, "Am I my kids' parent or their best friend?" And the answer that most helps you get through the challenges of these parenting years should be "yes" (see the upcoming chapter "Best Friend or Parent"). Kids need law and order now more than ever, but they also need your friendship and love more than ever—a tricky balancing act.

MILESTONE 13. FIFTEEN YEARS TO 18 YEARS—LETTING GO (STAGE 2)

Now is the time for parents to develop nerves of steel—nothing else will get you through your child's driver's license. Driving is your child's pre-launch. Although their most dramatic declaration of independence will occur as you say goodbye at their dorm room or apartment a few short years from now, driving is nature's way of easing parents into the idea of their kids leaving home. No longer needed to chauffeur or accompany, your challenge now is to adjust to the new reality of having near-grown kids. You'll go to bed before they do, so ask them to wake you to let you know they're home for the night.

MILESTONE 14. EIGHTEEN YEARS AND BEYOND

This parental milestone deserves a whole section of the book unto itself. See Part 3.

3D Parenting

There are days where it seems that all you do is get frustrated with your kids and fail to find your parental equilibrium. Of course you know what you're supposed to do. You're supposed to be a role model of reason and patience. Wise and understanding, yet firm and principled. And then they'll throw a temper tantrum when you're late for work, fight with their siblings for the "best" seat at the dinner table, beg for candy in the supermarket line, and refuse—absolutely refuse—to change their clothes, brush their hair, or eat their dinner.

Those are the times when parents often resort to 3D parenting: distraction, distortion, and deception. Yes, sometimes these may be necessary evils, the price of doing the business of parenthood. You really need your kids to do something NOW!, go somewhere FAST!, or just LEAVE YOU ALONE! for a few minutes. So you exaggerate the urgency, hyperbolize their intransigence, say mean things you don't mean, make deals and promises you know you'll never keep, or put them in front of the TV rather than hear one more whiny protest. I know, I've been there. This is not a holier-than-thou sermon, I promise.

Here's the problem with those 3Ds: your kids lose their trust in you. Not all at once, and not if you slip into the Ds only once in a while, dealing with your kids honestly and without sleight of hand most of the time. But gradually, the more you resort to distraction, distortion, and deception, the less strong the bond of trust between you and your kids. The result? They will be more likely to distract, distort, and deceive in their relationship with you as they grow older.

There's a solution to this problem. Replace those dark Ds with a set of three good and healthy Ds: defer, decompress, and deliver. At the height of tension and frustration, when you've simply got to be somewhere or get something accomplished, and when you feel your inner barometer rising, don't deal with the deeper issues. Defer them to later that day, decompress the immediate crisis, and then deliver on your promise to resolve the issue under calmer circumstances. Your kids will get the message that you respect them, take their feelings seriously, and can be taken at your word. No trickery just to get through the crisis—rather an honest commitment to fix the problem together. Later.

By the time later comes around, make sure you don't forget your pledge. Although by then, because kids really do live in the moment, they may have completely forgotten the earlier crisis du jour. Call your child into a quiet spot (see "Come into My 'Office'" in Part 2), sit next to each other, and offer to discuss whatever was upsetting her and whatever was upsetting you. How much better is this quality time together, calmly discussing the issue, than the time you would have wasted earlier in the day had you continued the struggle? When you realize how short the time we have with our kids really is, how many of those precious minutes, days, and weekends do you want lost to battles of wills and wars of words?

If she is still bothered when you meet later that day, work to fix it with her. If she has moved on, tell her you love her; tell her how you expect her to handle the next upset (remember, you are the parent and it's your job to teach correct behavior). And then move on with her.

Guilt and Worries

*P*arenting is among the greatest sources of human joy; it is also the single greatest cause of guilt and worry. Not only do we feel guilty about the things we've done or not done for our kids from the time they were born, but we also feel guilty about the genes we've burdened our kids with before they were born. And we worry about everything we can and can't control in our kids' lives. So there it is. Whatever our kids become or fail to become, achieve or fail to achieve, is our responsibility. Their health and happiness, sense of self, respect for others, and the course they chart for their lives all rest on our shoulders. Or so it seems. Whenever she would see a newborn, my grandmother would ask rhetorically, in her gentle European accent, "From this they have to make a person?"

It's impossible to fully alleviate you of your sense of guilt. Beginning with your baby's first diaper rash, you'll assume it's your fault for not changing her frequently enough. And it's downhill from there. And then there's the worry. Will they be happy and healthy and make wise choices? Will fate smile fondly on them? Will they associate with the right people? Have you taught them how to handle all the difficult and dangerous situations that will come up in their lives?

Here's the good news. By practicing *No Regrets Parenting*, you are hereby completely absolved of one form of guilt. No, not for the diaper rash. You are absolved of any guilt you might feel about not spending enough time with your kids. *No Regrets Parenting* is about opportunities, many realized, but some missed. If you find the minutes to do even a fraction of the suggestions in this book, you will have captured precious moments that would otherwise have been lost. And if you do more than a fraction of the suggestions? When the long days with your young kids are over, the years will not have seemed quite so short.

This is very important, so please read it carefully: You should never feel guilty about the minutes you can't spare, the times when you are too busy, and the moments that are lost to the realities of life despite your best efforts. *No Regrets Parenting* doesn't ask you to be perfect or superhuman; it only asks that you set the right priorities for your time and make the conscious effort to be there for your kids as often as possible. To help you with that, try the ideas in Part 2 of this book. Some may work for your family; others won't. Along the way, you'll invent your own strategies for turning scarce minutes into cherished moments. The only guilt you should ever feel is from not trying.

And here's another reason not to feel guilty. Kids need to grow their independence. Whenever you start to feel badly about leaving them with the babysitter, or dropping them at a friend's house where the friend's parent supervises the playdate, or putting them in front of the TV while you pull the house together, STOP THE GUILT TRIP! You're not neglecting them or failing as a *no regrets* parent because you're not with them 24/7. Rather, you're providing balance between the time they spend with you and the time they need away from you to develop independence. And kids need to know they don't have a claim on all of your time—the goal of *No Regrets Parenting* is appreciative kids and fulfilled parents, not spoiled kids and guilt-ridden parents.

What about the worries? So much of parents' worry is rooted in whether their kids are adequately prepared for the challenges they will face in their lives. *No Regrets Parenting* should ease some of that worry, too. The more time you spend with your kids, the more they see how you confront challenges and deal with life's uncertainties, the better they will understand from you how to set priorities in their own lives, and the less you will have to worry about.

Here's my bumper sticker for you: Be the kind of person you hope your kids will become. And then spend enough time with them that they learn how to become that person.

There are three kinds of worries in the world: kid worries, grown-up worries, and worries that are completely out of anyone's hands (the weather, for example). Kids should worry only about kid worries and leave the grown-up worries to their parents. Parents should worry only about those things that are within their control. *No Regrets Parenting* gives you more control over many of the worries you have for your kids. With your love, your time, and your role-modeling for them, you can sleep better knowing you have given them the foundation they need for the challenges that will come.

And as for those worries over which we truly have no control? It won't help to worry about them, so don't.

One of my favorite recent internet memes shows the silhouettes of a mom walking with her young daughter. The "thought bubbles" over the mom's head are full of worry: Am I a good enough mother? Why do other mothers seem to be so much more together than me? Are my kids happy? Are they learning enough from me? Do I spend enough time with them? But there's only a single thought bubble over the little girl's head: "I love her."

Milestone Madness

omparing your kids to others is natural—and one of the greatest sources of stress and worry in young parents' lives. My wife and I used to joke that when our kids were young, they were the only non-gifted, non-talented kids in school because everyone else's kids seemed to get tested and labeled "GT." Our kids just went to school, most times happily, sometimes grumpily, and did their work (most of the time). We never had them tested, always hoping they'd find their own comfortable zones for achievement without a label that separated them from their friends and classmates. As young adults today, they all seem to have turned out okay, despite never having been officially designated as special (except by us, of course).

Inevitably, in day care and preschools everywhere today, as was true yesterday and will be tomorrow, parents are watching the other kids to see how their own stack up. Developmental milestones are the most common measuring sticks. As everyone knows, children are supposed to roll over at three months, sit at six months, walk at one year, potty train at two years, ride a tricycle at three years, and get their driver's license at sixteen years. Right? Wrong. Well, maybe the driver's license milestone is right depending on which state you live in and how brave you are as a parent, but the rest are not nearly as predictable as developmental milestone charts would have you believe. Child development is a continuum, a gentle ramp or incline, not a series of discrete steps on a staircase. Although the differences between a six-month-old and a six-year-old are very dramatic, the differences between a six-month-old and an eight-month-old are much less so. Some kids walk at nine months, others at fifteen months or later. That doesn't predict their future SAT scores or athletic scholarships.

Anyone who's ever looked at the fine print on a board game (those are the games that come in boxes instead of on digital devices) knows that just because Candy Land says recommended for three- to five-year-olds, and Monopoly is recommended for kids eight years and older, doesn't mean that three-year-olds will like Candy Land or seven-year-olds won't beat you in Monopoly. Even board-game development is a continuum.

One of the great wonders of childhood is its unpredictability. Kids will surprise you, and surprise their pediatricians like me, with their unique progress through the developmental milestones. Your three-year-old is not delayed or abnormal just because he hasn't shown the least bit of interest in a tricycle (nor is she gifted and talented just because she rode a tricycle at two years and eight months). Of course, if you have concerns about your child's developmental progress, speak with his doctor, but don't obsess about the timing of each milestone. Kids have a way of finding their own pace and following the beat of their own drummer.

That said, there are four milestones worth mentioning, not because you should worry if they come a month or a year before or after they "should," but because these four milestones represent the emerging independence of your child.

Read on.

The Four Independence Days of Childhood

There are four milestones that launch kids from one stage of their young lives to the next, bringing them ever closer to their own independence. These are milestones for parents as well since each new step your kids take toward independence means a new phase in your lives as well.

INDEPENDENCE DAY #1—FIRST STEPS
Rolling from front to back, back to front, creeping, and then crawling are all big news in the life of a baby and her parents, and certainly cause for collecting video memories—but there is no mobility milestone that matches walking for excitement and a sense of accomplishment in the minds of parents and kids. Just watch the face of a baby hurtling upright from one parent to another, albeit a mere three feet away. And just watch the faces of the parents! And don't stop watching, because in the blink of an eye, walking becomes running, jumping, hopping, and skipping, and then good luck keeping track of them at the mall. That's independence!

INDEPENDENCE DAY #2—FIRST DAY OF SCHOOL
For some kids, this may be half- or all-day preschool; for others, kindergarten; but for all kids, that first time standing at the door of a classroom and saying goodbye to Mommy or Daddy is huge. It may involve clinging to Mom's leg for dear life. Or, it could mean a quick kiss and running off to meet new friends and find new toys, leaving

Mom and Dad wishing for a little more clinging. Vive la différence! Either way, all-day school will become part of your family's life for many years to come, and this first day is a true marker of independence from the comfort and security of home.

INDEPENDENCE DAY #3—DRIVER'S LICENSE

Many parents are taken by surprise at the impact their child's driver's license makes on the life of their family. When kids can get themselves to school and the mall, and take their younger siblings to soccer practice, a parent's first thought may be, "Hey, my life just got easier." And then it hits you: now they can go just about anywhere they choose, and pick up friends along the way, and use their cell phone in the car, and drive at night. And what if someone brings beer, and what if they do the stuff in the car that you did when you were their age?! What about all those other drivers on the road who may not be as conscientious as your kid?! Suddenly you, the chauffeurs of the past sixteen years, become terrified bystanders as your former dependents become freewheeling independents. This is the most telling independence day of all for kids and will say more about who they are than almost anything else they do along the way to adulthood. Driving brings so many opportunities to make good decisions, and such high risks for making bad ones. Buckle up!

INDEPENDENCE DAY #4—HIGH SCHOOL GRADUATION

And then it's here. After eighteen years, 940 weeks of childhood, they're up and out. Or, even if they're staying home for a while, they're officially young adults (much more about this phase of your parenting in Part 3). Old enough to vote and fight in wars. Old enough to say "no" without getting sent to their rooms. This is Independence with a capital "I,"—time to see your kids for the wonderful people they've turned into. Time to respect their opinions and decisions, no matter how much you may disagree. But don't panic. After your eighteen years of *No Regrets Parenting*, if all goes well, soon they'll begin respecting your opinions and your decisions, too. By the time the "fog of adolescence" lifts in their early twenties, your kids will be your new best friends. Friends you will want to be around and who will want to hang with you again. Really. Much more about you and your adult children in Part 3.

Your Legacy

What will your kids remember about their childhood—and about your role in it? My wife's grandmother was famous for periodically telling her daughters, "Remember, girls, you're having a happy childhood." What will your legacy be when your kids tell their kids about you?

Leave your kids with warm, glowing, and loving memories of the time they spent with you. When they leave for college or career, and other adult pursuits, they should be able to look back and recall the intimacy and depth, the laughter and lessons, the traditions and values of their relationship with you. They should feel so connected to you that they strive to use the same formulas and strategies that you used with them to create permanent and indelible bonds with their own kids. How thrilling it will be for you as a grandparent someday to hear your words coming from your child, now speaking to her own kids! Of course, your kids will do an even better job with their kids than you did with yours—isn't that the point?

Most importantly, your legacy depends on your kids really knowing you. That can happen only if they spend enough meaningful time with you to hear what you think, see what you do, and learn what you have to teach.

YOUR JOURNAL

A meaningful way to preserve your legacy as a parent—not only for your kids (and grandkids!) but also for you—is to keep a journal. Someday, as you flip back through the journal, you'll recall moments with your kids which may otherwise have been lost in the blur of daily parenting. Journals are a wonderful way of preserving your kids' "firsts," memorable things they said, and your favorite outings with them. You may ask: How can I possibly find time to journal—by the time the kids are asleep, I'm too exhausted to even hold a pen. Your entries needn't be elaborate essays, creative masterpieces, or a memoir in the making. A simple list of the week's memories with your kids will suffice. Or you may prefer a photo journal. Add photographs to your text for a more vivid memory.

If you just don't have enough energy left at the end of the day or week to journal your young kids' childhoods . . . ask their grandparents to do it for you (see Part 4, "*No Regrets* Grand*parenting*")!

The Villagers

This may sound a little old-fashioned, but I believe that kids who get 100 percent from their parents turn out, on average, to be better adjusted, happier, and more satisfied adults. And the parents of those kids have the blessing of knowing that their kids' success is not a coincidence. An oft-quoted proverb says, "It takes a village to raise a child." Indeed, the community your kids experience can provide them with an important sense of belonging and stability. But, again, I plead guilty to old-fashionism. Even though many villagers may participate in your kids' formative years, you are their most important guidepost, mentor, and friend. Relying too heavily on others for those roles is risky and, ultimately, unfulfilling.

Your kids' village is diverse, unfocused, and conflicted in its priorities. First of all, every village has its idiots who may negatively impact your kids, either intentionally or unintentionally; you have to be there to undo their influence. Of course, there are many villagers who can positively impact your kids—day-care providers, playgroup parents, teachers, classmates, clergy, coaches, college counselors, etc. They each have their own well-meaning agendas for your kids. But you must be the filter, finding the right balance of influences so your kids get the right messages. The villagers also have worries and distractions to deal with in their own lives. None are committed to your kids wholly and solely. That's your job alone, and your privilege.

What Do Your Kids Need from You?

This is your pediatrician speaking. In the nearly four decades I have been working with parents and children, the two most frequently asked questions have been:

1. What do my kids need most from me?

2. What must I do to be a good parent?

And I'll ask a third question: What do your kids *not* need from you? I'll answer the third question first—your kids don't need perfection. There is no such thing as the perfect parent or perfect parenting. You'll make mistakes, you'll have misgivings, and you'll make mountains out of molehills. And yes, you'll have regrets. But that's all to be expected and doesn't make you a bad parent. That you are worried about your mistakes, misgivings, and made-up mountains shows you are a concerned, conscientious, and thoughtful parent. More evidence? You are reading this book! Now to the first two questions.

The answer to the first is simple, and the answer to the second is simpler still. Years of research in child development and growth have identified eight essential requirements for kids to become happy, successful, kind, and resilient adults. For all the research and all the scholarly writings, there are no surprises here—you already intuitively know these fundamentals of parenting. Your kids need:

SECURITY—Kids must feel safe and sound. This means providing them with basic survival needs: shelter, food, clothing, medical care, and protection from harm.

STABILITY—Ideally, a family remains together in a stable household throughout kids' childhoods. But even when that ideal breaks down, your child's life must be as little disrupted as possible. Stability also comes from community. Kids and families should be part of larger units to give them a sense of belonging and cultural continuity.

CONSISTENCY—Parents must synchronize their parenting. No "good cop, bad cop." Deliver a singular message to your kids as their parents, not separately. Consistency also means that important values are important values and should not be changed casually or for convenience.

EMOTIONAL SUPPORT—Parents' words and deeds must engender trust, respect, self-esteem, and, ultimately, independence in their kids. In many families, parents also provide spiritual guidance in accordance with their own beliefs and values.

LOVE—Specialists rightly say that unwavering demonstration and expression of love for your kids can overcome almost any parenting "mistakes" you might make. Even when your kids have disobeyed, angered, frustrated, and rebelled against you, they must know that you love them unconditionally and you will always love them.

EDUCATION—It is your obligation and your challenge to make sure your kids get the best possible education to ensure their futures. This, of course, includes school. But it also includes the invaluable lessons about life that you can provide during the time you spend together. They learn by what they hear you say and by what they see you do.

POSITIVE ROLE MODELS—It's hard to say enough about the importance of role-modeling. As parents, you are your kids' first and most important role models. In addition to everything they learn from you about being good kids and good people, they are also watching how you parent. An undercurrent of this book is that if you find a way to make the most of every precious moment you have with your kids, not only will you raise wonderful kids, but you also will be showing them how to be wonderful parents to your grandchildren someday (see Part 4). Kids parent the way they were parented. Show them how important your time with them is, and you will impact generations to come.

STRUCTURE—Rules, boundaries, and limits. Without them, kids are forced to be adults before they are ready, and they lose respect for you and other adults.

So, those are the eight essential requirements of kids. Now for the second question: What do you need to do to be a good parent? Easy— provide those eight essentials for your kids! How? With time, the miracle solution for most dilemmas of childhood and parenthood— and the basis for this book. Time spent with your kids, taken in fleeting minutes or leisurely hours, gives you the opportunity to provide your kids with security, stability, consistency, emotional support, love, education, role-modeling, and structure. The converse is also true—not spending enough or the right kind of time with your kids deprives them of some or all of their basic needs. Equally important, not spending enough or the right kind of time with your kids deprives you of the wonderful privileges of parenting.

Part 2 of this book is all about finding that time.

Your Report Card

There are no grades given for parenting. No honor roll announced, certificates awarded, or degrees granted. You don't have to prove your parenting prowess to anyone except yourself. Sure, your toddler may throw a fit or two in protest of your rules. Your teenagers will very likely weigh in, sometimes quite demonstrably, on your parenting skills. And your adult kids (see Part 3) will inevitably reflect on their childhoods and on your parenthood. But ultimately it's your opinion about your parenting that matters most, because you're the one who will walk past their empty rooms when they're grown and you're the one who will reminisce over their baby pictures on the wall. Not every day with your kids will be perfect; in fact, many days with your kids may be far from perfect. As we say in our house, some days you eat the bear, and other days the bear eats you. But your report card isn't a daily reckoning—it's a cumulative performance evaluation. And this is one of those rare situations where you grade your own final exam.

When you have the time and energy to look back, how will you feel about yourself, your parenting, and the years you had with your kids? How will your self–report card turn out? Will you lament the time wasted, the opportunities missed, and the special moments that passed you by? Or will you have peace of mind, knowing that you did everything in your power to be there with your kids, to be the best parent possible, to give your kids every ounce of you that you were able to share?

This is neither a blame game nor a guilt trip. Truth be told, your kids don't need you constantly around to develop into decent, accomplished, and grateful adults. And there are certainly circumstances where parents' best intentions and efforts don't turn out as hoped. Circumstances where nature trumps nurture, or where twists and turns of life that are out of your control take your kids in the wrong direction. But even then, if you have made the most of your time with your kids and given everything you have to give, you'll never have to ask, "Was there more I should have done?"

When you take the red pencil to grade your final exam, make sure you'll be able to write in bold letters across the top: *no regrets.*

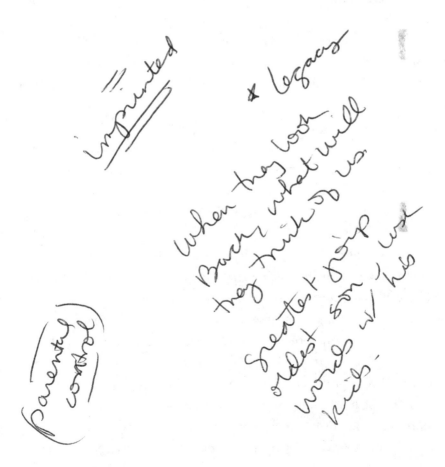

A New Type of "Quality Time"

 usy, working parents have often compensated for having so little quantity of time to spend with their children by invoking "quality time." Quality time usually means brief and choreographed bursts of activity dedicated intensively and exclusively to the kids—and when those bursts expire, the kids are turned over to the TV, video games, or the babysitter. Two hours at the nature preserve. An afternoon at the theater. Dinner at a fancy restaurant. That kind of quality time is often pricey because parents' expectations for those minutes with their kids are so high. Black and white: it's time with the kids, or it's time without the kids. This book, though, will show you the grays and redefine quality time for busy, working parents. Time at work needn't be devoid of kid time, and time at home may involve work, but both settings can include your kids in ways that benefit everyone, and both can help define a new quality time.

Professional lives spent moving up the ladder of success, or even treading water to maintain financial stability, have left little time for coddling and cuddling. Two-career family situations are especially hard on the quantity of time available for home life, making the quality time option of short, structured spurts of time with the kids seem like the only alternative. Adult responsibilities are realities. I will not advise you to handcuff your professional life or sacrifice your financial security "for the sake of the kids"—although you may choose to make some of those compromises because your priorities guide you in that direction. But you don't have to give up being a successful grown-up to be a successful parent. Rather, Part 2 of this book will show you how to make the most of every minute you do spend with your kids, and how to include the kids in more of your minutes than you may have thought possible. Quality time needn't be expensive; in fact, as you'll read in the upcoming chapter on money, the best experiences with your kids are usually free.

All the strategies for the new quality time that follow in Part 2 of this book need to be put into an age-appropriate context, where common sense rules. Most of the suggestions can be adapted and modified to fit the ages of your kids—kitchen duty, for example. At the youngest ages, sharing quality kitchen time with your kids may mean your infant finger-feeding himself Cheerios in the high chair while you cook, but helping you cook will come with growth (see also, the Epilogue—"My Favorite Letter"). The actual activity you and your kids share together is much less important than the togetherness you share in all of these activities.

So, let's agree that from this page forward, the new quality time means meaningful and memorable time, regardless of duration or content. Quality time may occur when you least expect it—yes, at the nature preserve, but also in the minivan on the way to ballet practice and during the commercials of your favorite family TV show. Although you may use your newfound quality time for teaching your kids life lessons, addressing their crises, or planning the upcoming weekend, most of the quality time you discover in this book is unscripted and spontaneous. By the time the kids are in college or in their first real jobs, quality time may have to be phone or texting time on their way between classes or meetings (see Part 3). Even then, unscripted and spontaneous is important. When our oldest left for college, there were so many things we needed to hear about when he called, and so much advice and encouragement we felt we needed to give him, that we forgot about unscripted and spontaneous time. Until he reminded us—"Guys, can we just talk about baseball for a few minutes? How 'bout that Colorado Rockies shortstop?!"

The purpose of Part 2 of this book is to guide you in creating ample opportunities for new quality time with your kids, despite your hectic lives and chaotic schedules. And when you accomplish that goal, your kids' next birthdays won't seem to have passed as quickly.

Subliminal Togetherness

The more time you spend with your kids, taking advantage of every precious moment, the less time they are on their own, learning lessons of independence. Kids need plenty of time alone and with friends to explore their environment and to establish their identities. Yet, they also need lots of time with you to learn how to explore and establish. They learn by watching you, listening to you, and imitating you. This presents a real conundrum for parents wanting to slow down the years without slowing down their child's maturation.

So . . . how can you achieve a healthy balance with your kids between independence and togetherness? How can you avoid "helicopter" (drone!) parenting, hovering around them all the time, while still enjoying as much time together as you can squeeze in before they're off on their own?

The "Calendars" section in Part 2 of this book guides you in using your kids' schedules to help set your own—prioritizing their events and their schedules and trying to work your commitments around theirs so you can be there for the important adventures in their lives. But, although your goal should be to never miss their big karate match or class play, you should miss those times in your kids' lives when they need space to grow and learn on their own. School, of course, gives them plenty of time away from you—but those hours are highly programmed and less amenable to independent exploration.

Give your young kids downtime with toys or TV when they come home from school, and plenty of playdates with friends where you, or their friends' parents, are in another room keeping an eye and ear on them from a distance. Let them play and explore in the fenced backyard where you can see them through the windows, and at the playground with you watching from the nearby park bench. Youth sports programs help your kids develop independence and social skills. At the right age, and with appropriate safeguards, wandering on the internet and social media is a very "today" version of independence. When they're adolescents, the closed door to their rooms should be respected—privacy for teens must be indulged and endured by parents, within limits, of course. Separation times like these also give you "sanity breaks."

But the best of all worlds are those situations where your kids can be independent, with you at their sides or in their shadows. Let's call this shared-but-separate state of being subliminal togetherness. The idea is that you and your kids are sharing new and interesting experiences without your kids feeling your presence or being subjected to your real-time interpretations and lessons. They form their impressions and learn from their environment, without your influence. Or at least without your influence being obvious. Your kids' first rafting trip is a similar experience for them whether you are also on the raft or they go with friends. You get to see your kids' first trip down the river and can talk about it with them on the car ride home, but the excitement and energy they feel is all their own. Or their first lemonade stand, with you supervising from the living room window, available for consultation and replenishment of ice as needed. "Hire" your child as "mom's helper," letting him look after younger siblings or neighbors' kids while you're elsewhere in the house taking care of your chores and listening in as your child grows into his new responsibilities; this is a great time to dust off the baby monitor you used when they were in their cribs and playpens. Train the new puppy with your kids—they'll be so excited about teaching their pet that they won't notice that you are teaching them how to teach, and then take the dog for walks together. Help coach your child's sports team or be the scoutmaster for their scouting troop, participating side-by-side with them without restricting the growth and maturation they get from being part of a team. When your kids are old enough to have driving permits, drive with them as often as you can. They will be so excited and terrified to finally be driving a car that they'll barely notice you—that is, until you scream that they just ran a red light! Subliminal togetherness.

As your kids get older, their truly independent time will quickly increase, and your together time with them will just as quickly decrease. They'll go on the raft trip without you, exchange their lemonade stand for a real summer job, grow from "mom's helper" to full-fledged babysitter, and replace their learner's permit with a real driver's license. All of that is as it should be, and all the more reason to make the most of your time together at all ages of their childhood.

One-on-One, Zone Defense, and "Can I Bring a Friend?"

*E*verything gets more complicated when your formerly only child has a sibling. One-on-one time with each child is important. For the older sibs, it lets them know you still care about their interests and are proud of the new abilities they have developed. It tells them that having younger siblings is not going to ruin their lives, steal their parents, or dumb down their days. And one-on-one time with your younger kids gives them a chance to be the bigshots in a household where older sibs often rule. It tells them they are not just a shadow, always tagging along wearing inherited clothes. Another benefit of one-on-one time is the decompression it brings to the natural sibling rivalry kids often feel. When you're with your kids one at a time, there's no competition for your attention and, as long as the other kids know they'll get their turns, there's no resentment for spending time with only one.

If you are a two-parent family, one-on-one time is straightforward with two kids; after that you shift into zone defense with each parent at times covering more than one child. If you're a single-parent family with more than one child, zone defense is standard. Even in zone, though, you should try to find quality time for each child separately. Not necessarily every day and not with every activity. On some days, for part of the day, break away from the others and make special memories with one child. That, of course, means you need to find a grandparent, babysitter, or playdates for the others, but they'll get their turn, too.

Now that we are preserving as many minutes and moments for you and your kids as possible, where do friends fit in? The last thing we want to result from family time is for your kids to return to school after quality time with you and find themselves in a clique of one. So, two new dilemmas—do we take friends along on our outings, and do we give up our kids to other families who invite them as playmates for their kids?

The answer to both questions is "yes." And "no." Of course your kids need friends to be happy and accepted and to develop social skills. But they need you more. And as your kids get older, their time with friends—in school, after school, and even on weekends—will increase logarithmically. As hard as it may be to believe when your kids are very young, you'll have to compete for their time very soon. So here's the way I would prioritize your family time when the issue of friends comes up—as it often will and should.

1. First choice is time with you.

2. When it's important to your kids to have a friend, or important for a friend to be with your kids, include the friend in some of your activities while still preserving some time that day for just you and your kids.

3. Since the parents of your kids' friends are also reading this book, they are going to want to host your kids for part of their family time. This is only fair, and sometimes you'll have to lend your kids out to others. Use the time when your child is with a friend's family to arrange one-on-one time with your other kids or to catch up on work that you would otherwise have to do when the kids are asleep. That way, you'll be swapping family time rather than giving it away, and you'll have more time for your

kids after dinner than you had expected. Oh, and yes, it's okay to also use the time your kids are away with a friend for "me" time. You've earned some of that, too (see the upcoming "Staying Sane" chapter).

Best Friend or Parent?

*A*re you your kids' best friend or are you their parent? Many have written about the risks of being your children's best friend—overindulgence, underdiscipline, failure to set limits or establish structure in your kids' lives. Those admonitions are true. We can never lose sight of our parenting responsibilities, even when those put us into the bad-guy role, which they frequently do.

But this is another one of those situations in which it's not either/or—we should always be our kids' best friends, too. Each parent is *both* good cop and bad cop—those roles should never be divided up between two parents. Never be afraid to scold if doing so teaches and protects your kids. Don't shy away from disciplining kids—they have to, and want to, respect you even if they "hate" you for a few minutes for telling them no. But as necessary as the bad cop is, the good cop is even more important for you and for your kids. By being there during their big moments and little moments alike, making sure they have plenty of belly laughs and giggles, and being available to patiently advise and teach, we show our kids they can trust us not just as parents, but as friends. Best friends.

The more we know about our kids' lives, the more valuable we become when they have worries or crises. We know their friends' names and which kids are the school bullies; we know the quirks of our kids' teachers, the lunchroom menu, and the schedule for student council elections. Soon enough, friends their own age will become your kids' confidants and consultants—but when that transition occurs, the close relationships you have built with your kids will bring them back to you for the big issues and even for some of the smaller ones. When your kids feel you are actively engaged in their lives, because you have had ample time with them to truly listen and absorb, they will feel comfortable entering into each new discussion with you—they won't feel that "you just don't get it, Mom," because you do get it. You know the players and the play, so each new scene starts in a familiar setting.

That's what being a best friend is all about.

Designer Children—Nature vs. Nurture

You want your kids to be smart, talented, kind, responsible, well mannered, loving, athletic, humble, generous, funny, and good-looking, right? Not a problem. There are hundreds of books and websites out there to help with each of those child designs and more. *Raising a Studious Child, Creating Nicer Kids, Teaching Your Children to Love, Growing Your Child's Natural Talents, The Well-Groomed Child Within, Taming the Stubborn Child, Liberating the Shy Child,* etc. Of course, I made up those titles, and any resemblance to actual child-design books is purely accidental. But you get the point. Many gurus will tell you how to mold, fix, and tailor your kids into the perfect little angels, or robots, you are hoping for. I'm not smart enough to be able to do that, so I have a much simpler, two-step approach:

> **FIRST STEP**—Embrace nature. Teach your kids to accept and be grateful for the gifts nature gave them. Every child is born with a genetic "package," over which he or she has no choice. One of our most poignant moments with our daughter was a teary one, sitting with her on the edge of her bed, six years old, discussing "packages." Sure, sweetheart, there might be things you would change about yourself if you could. There are the things Mommy and Daddy were born with that they like a lot, and there are the things Mommy and Daddy got in their "packages" that they don't like as much—or even hate, sometimes. And your best friend whom you really wish you

could look more like? When you look at her *whole* "package," are you sure you really want to be her? Look at all the wonderful things you got in your "package" that you would never, ever change. Aren't you glad you're you?

SECOND STEP—Provide nurture. Be the type of person you want your children to become, and then spend plenty of time with them so they can learn from your role modeling. After your kids are born, tiny "packages" of natural gifts, the world around them takes over, nurturing and determining the kind of people they will be. Parents are the most important nurturers in their kids' worlds, and the most influential in shaping their future selves. Children are sponges, soaking up conscious and unconscious lessons that you teach them.

Design your children well, by your example.

Brain Buttons

I am a physician, but what I'm about to tell you is not based on anatomy or neurobiology or medicine. It's based on my experience as a parent and my observations of the kids and parents I've cared for over the past four decades. Kids' brains are too cluttered, chaotic, cloudy, and complicated to properly register most of what you are trying to communicate to them most of the time. Your kids' eyes may be open, but often there's nobody home. While you're hoping they are absorbing the pearls of wisdom you're dispensing, they are zoned out in a parallel universe where they keep doing the same nonsensical and illogical things despite your repeated teaching, preaching, and beseeching. Teaching, preaching, and beseeching are important, to be sure. But for effective *No Regrets Parenting*, there is a secret for permanently imprinting your kids' brains with the lessons you are teaching them, and with wonderful feelings and memories of their time with you. How is that possible if your kids are in perpetual brain freeze?

The best way to cut through the fog in their brains and reach your kids' centers of understanding and appreciation is by pushing their three hidden attention buttons. First, the "fun button." Kids start to pay attention, and therefore are better able to learn and remember, when they are enjoying themselves. It's as if their brains don't want to miss any of the fun, so they lock in on whatever is going on while they're having fun. Enjoying themselves is what kids do for a living, so this strategy for getting through to them is easy. If you want them to learn about safely crossing the street, teach them on the way to the ice cream store or the amusement park. Not only will they learn to look both ways, but they'll also remember that you made learning fun and yummy. What a great parent you are! More importantly, you remember how much fun being a parent can be and how vital what you have to teach your kids is for their safety and for their future.

Don't forget to laugh with your kids—boisterous, booming belly laughs. Laughter bonds like no other activity in life. Laughter boosts your immune system (trust me, I'm a doctor) and extends your life (trust me, same reason). Laughter pushes your kids' "fun button," helping them focus and listen to you. Be goofy, play practical jokes, tickle, watch slapstick movies. Learn magic tricks to amaze your kids and their friends; turn the sprinkler on them; dress up in funny clothes or silly hats to surprise them. There's nothing like hearing your kids tell their friends, "This is my dad—he's funny!" And while they (and you) are having fun, they are more receptive than ever to what you are trying to teach them.

Another underappreciated attention switch in your kids' brains is their "audit button." It's flipped on whenever they watch you in your daily activities: working, driving, cooking, cleaning, playing, relaxing, speaking, and showing your love. If you don't think your kids are scrutinizing what you do, try uttering a curse word or throwing a dish in a fit of anger. Your behavior will be mimicked and your poorly chosen words parroted. Politeness, affection, pride, confidence, patience, tolerance, morality, respect, and self-control will also be mimicked. Our youngest child's first complex sentence came when he was sitting in his car seat, running errands with Mom. He was holding a toy plastic phone, put it to his ear, and said, "Driving car pool, be little late." When people say how much your kids remind them of you, make sure that's a compliment.

You turn on the "mosey button" in your kids' brains when you s . . . l . . . o . . . w   d . . . o . . . w . . . n. We overload our kids, and ourselves, with the deadlines and dance card of each day. Kids can't lock in or focus when they're rushing. Set aside daily moseying time. Mosey through dinner; mosey for an evening walk after dinner; mosey during story time. The extra few minutes you devote to eating slower, walking slower, and reading slower will give your kids' brains a breather and let them better appreciate their time with you, and vice versa. It's true that just being able to gather everyone at the same table for dinner is often a difficult feat, and after-dinner commitments feel pressing. But chew a little slower and linger a little longer—even fifteen extra minutes can make the difference between a "functional" dinner and an enjoyable family event. Stretch the bedtime story a few minutes longer, too. If you're looking at your watch while you're reading to your kids, they'll sense the rush and you will lose the magic of the moment.

It's especially important to mosey during listening time, whenever that occurs in your kids' day; it's so important that there's a whole chapter coming up about listening. As hard as it may be sometimes, try not to rush your kids when they're telling you about their day, their accomplishments, or their worries. Give them your undivided attention—you won't have to do it for long because they'll tire of talking and move on to their next activity. But while they are in a sharing mood, share.

Traditions

Russian scientist Ivan Pavlov became famous at the turn of the twentieth century for discovering and characterizing what he called the "conditioned reflex." Simply put, if dogs became accustomed to hearing a bell ring immediately before he fed them, soon the dogs began to anticipate their meal, salivating at the sound of the bell before ever seeing or smelling the food. That's the way traditions begin; those dogs probably told their puppies to listen carefully for ringing bells because of the wonderful things that happen when that occurs.

Traditions are conditioned reflexes. Throughout Part 2 of this book, you will find suggestions for establishing family traditions that will trigger happy anticipation and leave lasting, cherished memories. Traditions around major holidays and minor holidays. Bedtime, bath time, and mealtime traditions; sports and hobby traditions; birthday and anniversary traditions; charitable and educational traditions.

If your family's traditions coincide with others' observances, such as celebrating Thanksgiving, you can still make those traditions unique to your family with the personal nuances you add. Volunteering at the food bank on Thanksgiving morning, measuring and marking their heights on the door frame in the basement, Grandpa's artistic carving of the turkey, and their uncle's famous gravy are the traditions our kids salivated about when they were younger, and still do on their long plane rides home at the end of November each year. (By the way, our beloved late dog Lizzy confirmed Pavlov's observations; when the carving knife turned on, cue the saliva, tail-wagging, and doggy squealing.)

But don't limit your family's traditions to the big and obvious events like Thanksgiving. Weekly taco nights, family book club and movie nights, pajama walks, ice cream sundaes on Sundays, backyard football during halftime of TV games, pancakes in Mom and Dad's bed on weekends, leaf fights in the fall, walks to the sledding hill on the season's first snow, Chinese food on anniversaries, Indian food for other big occasions, and balloons hanging from the ceiling around the breakfast table on birthday mornings. Be creative, even silly. Make a secret family noise together when you're the only ones in the elevator. When you share a secret that "can't leave this room," everybody knows to reach up in the air and grab the imaginary tidbit before it can get away. Have a family comedy night or a talent show on each birthday. Make holiday cards from scratch. Celebrate major family events by writing personalized lyrics to an old song and karaoke-ing your new composition together.

There are two keys to establishing family traditions: repetition and anticipation. When you find something that brings out excitement and smiles in your kids, keep doing it. Not so often that it becomes mundane, but on a regular and predictable enough basis that it becomes an ingrained part of the family repertoire. And begin talking about the traditional event days ahead of time so by the time it finally happens, your kids are beside themselves with excitement. Anticipation can be as much fun as the tradition itself.

The Parenting Meditation

By now you have realized that turning scarce minutes into cherished moments, and redefining quality time, are our goals. You're trying hard to be there for big events and small events, creating enduring traditions and lifelong memories. But here's a disturbing truth. Even if you attempt the impossible—doing everything I recommend in Part 2 of this book—it won't be enough. Unless you are really paying attention. Paying attention to your kids' childhoods, and to your parenthood, will be the toughest assignment I give you.

As Far Eastern customs and culture have found their way to those of us in the West, meditation and mindfulness have become familiar to many. But even if you've heard the terminology, and even if you've tried the practice, you probably have never considered applying them to parenting. But *No Regrets Parenting* requires its own special form of mindfulness and meditation.

Here's the reason. I hope that, perhaps with the help of this book, you will quickly learn to navigate family life and schedules well enough to salvage substantial time with your kids that otherwise would be lost in the everyday mayhem and madness. That's the good news. The bad news is that you may be so overwhelmed with the responsibilities and complexities of parenthood that you toggle into autopilot, oblivious to the wonders you have created. If your mind is elsewhere during the precious moments that you have worked so hard to preserve, you have lost your kids' childhoods just as sure as if you hadn't spent the time with them at all.

And it's easy for that to happen. With your kids in the kitchen helping you make dinner, your mind is taking you back to this morning at the office, or pushing you ahead to tomorrow's busy agenda. By the time you realize that you've zoned out, dinner is finished and the kids are upstairs doing homework. What did they say to you? What did you answer? What are they worried about? Did you comfort them? Your walk in the park with them on a weekend morning is serene and soothing—unless you're still obsessing about the fight you had with your spouse, or about preparing your taxes, or paying your utility bill. When you get back, your kids dash off to play with friends, and you're not sure if you held hands with them on your walk, if you stopped at the playground, or even if you remembered to ask them about the bully who's been bothering them at school. You rush from work to get to their soccer game but don't notice them playing because you're thinking about what you didn't finish before you left. You film their birthday party but don't even see what the camera sees because you're thinking you should be cutting the lawn or fixing the car.

Sure, you can pat yourself on the back for involving the kids in dinnertime preparation, walking with them in the park, getting to their soccer practice, and being there for their birthdays—but why bother? You missed those events even though you were there!

The traditional practice of mindful meditation teaches how to clear your head of the torrents of distracting thoughts that constantly interject themselves, or at least to acknowledge the distractions and dismiss them. It's not easy. The most common approach is to focus on the involuntary act of breathing. By paying attention to something that usually requires no attention at all, despite occurring ten to twenty times every minute, the brain is given a focal point from which extraneous thoughts can be excluded. The goal is, in meditation jargon, "staying in the moment." Staying in the moment means that what's important is what is, right now, right here. The temptation to think back or project forward is great, but "now" is the focus of your attention.

Locking in on your breathing, the most consistent and reliable manifestation of "now," helps you stay in, and be mindful of, the moment. Ironically, kids are almost always much more "in the moment" than their parents—what matters to young kids is what's happening this minute, not what happened yesterday or is scheduled for tomorrow. As noted elsewhere in Part 1 of this book (see the earlier chapter on "3D Parenting" and the next chapter on "Listening"), that "now" attribute of kids comes in very handy in resolving many of their crises du jour.

So, how does mindful meditation apply to *No Regrets Parenting?* Taking a deep, settling breath during parenthood's chaos is always a good idea, but when you are with your kids, you can't simply tune everything out and focus on breathing while your kids are desperately asking for ice cream, advice, or the potty. But what you can do is a "parenting meditation" that requires a similar kind of focus. During the precious moments that you have protected to share with your kids, focus on seeing them, hearing them, understanding them, and being amazed by them. I mean *really* seeing every feature of them; *really* hearing every word they say and the tone they say it with; *really* understanding their hopes and wishes and concerns; and *really* being amazed by what you've created—living, breathing miracles of nature who are learning like sponges and growing like weeds. Stay in the moment when you have moments with your kids. During those often too brief interludes, your kids should be all that's happening and where it's at.

For some of you, this will mean really *noticing* your kids for the first time in weeks or months, maybe since the day you held them with awe in the delivery room. At the moment of their birth, they had your undivided attention. You registered every coo, cry, and gurgle; counted their fingers and toes; brushed their wispy hair with your fingers; and kissed them gently on their soft spots. At other momentous occasions, you probably paid pretty close attention, too. Her christening or his bris.The first day of preschool or kindergarten. The first steps they took or the first time balancing on a two-wheeler.

But how will you feel someday if the next time you really notice your child is at high school graduation, or on his wedding day? Stunned that it went by so quickly, puzzled by how you missed it even though you were physically there? Those are regrets; your job is to reach that day with *no regrets*. That requires paying attention to your kids on all the days in between the big occasions. Noticing them when you're driving them to school, when you read their bedtime story, while you're running through a rainstorm with them or building a snowman. What are your kids thinking? What are they asking? How did they get so cute and so smart?

I used a personal trick for meditating on my kids when they were young, and I use it on my grandkids now—I "channel." My father died young, before meeting my wife or my kids. When they were doing really cute things, or just looking really cute, I would focus on them intently, trying to somehow channel their images to my dad. That locked me in on my kids long enough to remind me how important truly noticing them was—I wanted my dad to "see" them, too, so I really concentrated on my kids. Now that my mom has died, I include her in my channeling of our adult kids and our grandkids.

Be "mindful" of your kids, and be dazzled by them. "Meditate" on their loose teeth and their skinned knees. Marvel as they play baseball or the piano. Be overcome with wonder at their wisdom and innocence. "Channel" if that helps you as it did me.

It is only by noticing your children that you will truly know your children.

Listening

*I*f you don't listen to your kids, really listen, your time together is wasted. Kids have silly worries and crazy ideas. Kids are immature and repetitive. Impulsive and emotional. They exaggerate and fabricate; they make mountains out of molehills. That may be the way you sometimes hear them, with your ears and your brain. But your kids think they are wise and insightful, mature, patient, and brilliant. Kids ask questions because they want answers—and because they want your attention. They want to hear you speak to them and teach them. Most importantly, kids are usually "in the moment" and believe their issues and concerns, right this minute, are all that matters (see the previous chapter). The mean thing her best friend said; his teacher's unreasonable new rules; the shove he got from the cute girl on the playground; the Valentine's note she wants to leave for her secret crush; the embarrassment he felt when you scolded him in front of his friends. As trite and non-urgent as these matters may sound to your adult ears and brain, they are front-page news for your kids.

Listen to your kids and treat their words with respect. Don't form your response in your head before you've heard their whole saga—if you do, you're not really listening. Hear "between the lines," because there may be important unspoken messages in their words. Let your kids know by your facial expressions, your patience, and your thoughtful response that you feel their pain and share their concerns. Don't ever make your kids feel that you think their worries are trivial. Don't tell your kids they'll understand how minor their issue is when they get older. Parent your kids, don't patronize them. While you know that by tomorrow, and maybe even by later tonight, the crisis du jour will have faded, *they* don't know that. Help them get through their crises as you would hope your spouse, partner, or close friend would help you get through yours. In this way, you will let your kids know that they can come to you when they're troubled, no matter the nature of the distress, and that you will be there for them. You're their closest friend. They won't have to go elsewhere for comfort, landing in the hands of people who love them a lot less than you do. You're always there, and your kids' problems are your problems, and you will solve them together. Then your kids will include you in their lives and in their bigger crises as they get older.

Our kids seemed to always remember their biggest crises as soon as we pulled into the school parking lot in the morning. As other kids were bounding out of cars all around us, there was always something really important that one or more of our kids needed to discuss. They had forgotten to tell us about the test today. Or to study for it. They had forgotten their homework at home. Or their lunch. Or that it was "silly hat day." Or that it wasn't "paint your face day." Oops. With the school bell about to ring, or when you're late for work, or when you're exhausted after a long day, it is hard to listen. But that's when you have to try the hardest to lock into your kids' soliloquies. They may be impossible to deal with right now—after all, the BELL *IS* RINGING and YOU *ARE* LATE FOR WORK! But give your kids your solemn pledge that you will listen, and you will have time tonight. Promise that you will listen to the whole story, beginning to end, as soon as you can. And if your kids know that you keep your promises to listen to them, and you think what they say is important, they will give you a pass until later.

NOW, GET OUT OF THE CAR AND INTO SCHOOL!!! Please. ☺.

Listening well to your kids has two other big perks, one obvious and one a bit more subtle. The obvious benefit is that you'll know what's going on in their brains and in their lives. We well remember the first time our kids came home from preschool with ideas of their own, notions they dreamed up without our planting them in their heads. Wow, what a revelation it is to hear your kids' original thoughts! As they grow older, their own thoughts and ideas come fast and furiously. They learn from teachers, friends, TV, the internet, and social media. Before you know it, you can lose track of what they're doing and what they're thinking about. Knowing your kids, really knowing them, requires patient listening. And it's by really knowing your kids that you will feel *no regrets* as the years streak by.

The more subtle benefit to careful listening is the perception you leave with your kids. The actual advice you give is often less important to them, and to the situation at hand, than is the true impression they will form of you: that you care about them and their predicaments. The solution that you might offer to any dilemma is rarely as important as the fact that you were there to work it through with them. That's like a no-fault guarantee. Even if you blow it, your kids know you gave it your best shot. That in and of itself is a nice lesson for them: my parents are human and may not always be right, but they tried to help me and were humble enough to admit when their advice was wrong or didn't work. You score big points for effort.

Staying Sane

So, because I wrote this rah-rah book about parenting, you think I must love every minute of the parenting experience. Wrong. Personal confession and full disclosure: it's not always easy, and it's not always enjoyable, to be with your kids. And sometimes, it's just awful. Depending on their ages, kids can be physically taxing and emotionally trying (hence the "long days" part of "long days, short years"). Part 2 of this book provides strategies for maximizing the time you have with your kids *during* your daily routine, before they grow up and *leave* your daily routine. Tips for squeezing in precious moments while you still can. On the other hand . . . when kids drive you nuts, they can really drive you nuts! So, how to find the right prescription for wonderful and plentiful time with your kids, without overdosing?

Here are four tips for maintaining your balance:

1. **DOUBLE DIP.** Young kids love being part of many adult activities—it makes them feel grown up. Gardening, cooking, baking, scrapbooking, fishing, snow-shoveling, leaf-raking, tinkering on your car. Pick activities that you and the kids would enjoy *without* each other, then do them together.

   There are many activities to keep you and your kids happy at the same time in Part 2 of this book. A few more examples:

BIKING—Put the littlest ones in a trailer and the somewhat older ones on a trailer cycle that hooks onto your bike and lets your child pedal; once kids are old enough to bike next to you, they get their own wheels. You get outdoor exercise, your kids get fresh air, and you get each other.

CHARITY—Do a charity walk together; get sponsors and spend a weekend day doing a healthy outdoor activity for a good cause. Or have a spring-cleaning day where everyone collects clothes and toys from the closets and under the beds to donate. Then go to the collection center together and demonstrate the act of giving for your kids to watch and learn from."

JOGGING—Strollers made for keeping your kids close while you're pounding the pavement are perfect for together times that relieve, rather than create, stress.

LANGUAGE LESSONS—Learn a second language together, listening to tapes on long car rides or in the dentist's waiting room. And then go online to explore the country and culture of people who natively speak that language (see "Speaking Their Language" in Part 2).

SWIMMING—The pool feels great on a hot day whether you're an adult or a kid. When the kids are old enough to play in the pool unsupervised, you can swim laps while they splash their friends.

READING—Books are one of the best ways to reconcile different attention levels and interests. Try quiet time with everyone reading their own latest page-turner.

2. **TAKE ADVANTAGE OF THEIR COMMITMENTS.** When the kids have activities that you can't share, use that time to escape from parenting and indulge yourself. Beginning with preschool, your kids' calendars start to fill up with blocks of hours to which you're not invited. These are vital growth opportunities for your kids—and for you! You've earned quality *adult* time and should feel no guilt taking that time for yourself when the kids are doing their thing. Sit in a coffee shop, go to the gym, stream your favorite series, take a bath, sneak in a rendezvous with your spouse or partner. The more you enjoy your time away from the kids, the less you'll feel burdened when you're all together again.

3. **PUT YOURSELF IN "TIME OUT."** Don't feel compelled to share *every* precious moment with the kids. When you've had enough, take a grown-up break and put the kids in front of the TV, let them play video games, or take them to Grandma's. Forcing yourself into nonstop togetherness with your kids will spoil them and may spoil your relationship with them. Absence, in limited quantities, can indeed make the heart grow fonder. Spend as much time as you can with your kids, but know when you need a breather, and take it. A quiet bath, glass of wine, comfort food snack, a walk on the treadmill, or a midday nap. You're not a bad parent because your kids are watching *Toy Story* for the fortieth time. This is especially important when your temper is about to flare, which it inevitably will do on occasion. Separate yourself from your kids until you're ready to calmly and comfortably reconnect. And don't feel guilty about it (see the earlier "Guilt and Worries" chapter).

4. **BE REALISTIC AND PACE YOURSELF.** If you try to do each and every one of the suggestions in Part 2 of this book, sanity is out of the question. You'll drive yourself and your kids up a wall if you use this book as an inviolable instruction manual for your lives. Rather, see this as a potpourri of ideas, some to try now, others for later; some may never be right for you and your family. You know the chemistry and physics of your household. If summer sleepaway camp is a mainstay for your family, ignore my advice for day camping. If you live in Manhattan, pajama walks after dinner (and during rush hour!) may be a stupid idea. Don't be a room parent or teacher's helper if your middle school kids are mortified by the thought of their friends seeing you in their classroom. Pick and choose from the menu of together times that make up this book, and you'll stay sane while still capturing precious moments with your kids that would otherwise be lost.

Money

$\mathcal{S}$ure, it helps. But there's nothing in this book that requires lots of money. In fact, every chapter in Part 2 can be tailored to your budget without detracting from the fun or fond memories. If the economy is in the potty, or your bank accounts are in recession, your discretionary money for travel, recreation, vacations, and restaurants may vanish. In addition, many parents find themselves scrambling to find extra work and extra sources of income to cover the costs that come with kids. That's potentially a perfect storm for disrupting your time with your kids—more time spent at work and less money to use during non-work time. It's times like those that test your creativity and ingenuity. This book is written to help you find the most creative and ingenious uses for both your time and your money.

Most of the suggestions for stretching the time with your kids are entirely free—they just need you. Anything in Part 2 that requires *any* money at all can be easily scaled to your means—your favorite family restaurant can be the fast-food place, the pancake place, or a more upscale establishment, depending on the priorities you set for family funds. To my mind, the cheaper and healthier the better. You may prefer family movie night to mean a trip to the theater at $10 per ticket—but movies are available on standard TV channels (where you have to put up with commercials); subscription streaming services (where you don't have to put up with commercials) often cost less for a full month of movie access for your whole family than one ticket at the theater.

One of the biggest mistakes you can make as a parent is to equate, in your own mind or in your kids' minds, the cost of a good time with the good time itself. It would be great if everyone could afford tickets to see the latest kids' musical theater or ice-skating extravaganza that comes to town. But if you can't, wait till the free theater-in-the-park programs start next summer, go to the nearby high school for its theater performances, or stream the movie version of the play. If the cost of seeing the hottest teen sensation in concert is prohibitive, record her next TV concert and watch with your kids. And if you *can* afford the tickets for musical theater, the ice-skating extravaganza, or the big concert, think twice about whether those are investments you should make; if they are, enjoy them to the fullest. But make sure your kids know these are rare treats, because there are many important things you need to save for, and many worthwhile causes to which you want to donate.

If you don't invest the time and effort to know your kids and to be an integral part of their lives, don't try to buy them off with expensive outings and activities—it won't work. The worst message you can send your kids is that you consider an expensive day out as an offset for the many inexpensive opportunities to be with them that you've missed (see the earlier chapter, "A New Type of 'Quality Time'"). Not only do you lose your irreplaceable time with them, but you also degrade their value system about what's important in life.

Beware Becoming the "Potpourri Parent"

This is a book about protecting precious moments and redefining quality time with your kids. It's a book about sifting through the responsibilities and commitments of everyday life and reclaiming more time to spend with your kids. Enough time to become an integral part of their lives, and enough time to make them the focal point of your life. But there are potential hazards that come with interwoven lives. If you're not mindful, you might *misuse* the time you've worked so hard to salvage.

It's natural for parents to hope for generational advancement—greater happiness and success for their kids than parents have attained for themselves. This can lead to a hyperbolic version of child-raising, for which I'll coin my own new term: "potpourri parents." These are parents who expose their kids to unprecedented opportunities for self-discovery and mentored accomplishments, in the hope that somewhere in the smorgasbord they will have an experiential epiphany, a sudden realization of their purpose and place. Potpourri kids have karate Mondays and tap dancing Tuesdays; play competitive tennis on Wednesdays (under the supervision of the club pro); get math tutoring after school on Thursdays; and have rehearsals for the school play on Fridays. Without the inconvenience of school to worry about, weekends are even more ambitiously choreographed, all with the parents' goal of getting their kids into the best private schools, colleges, internships, or careers someday.

By pushing their kids toward excellence, even superiority—in school, sports, music, theater, standardized tests, etc.—potpourri parents may neglect one of the most important obligations and thrills of parenting: letting kids be kids. The goal of *No Regrets Parenting* isn't limited to its benefits for parents. Kids must also be able to look back on their own childhoods without the regrets of growing up too fast, prematurely feeling adult pressures, and not having enough freedom to be kids.

Teach your kids resilience—ambition is good, but disappointments occur despite trying hard. Encourage them to be the best they can be in everything they do, but let them know they don't necessarily have to be better than everyone else in everything they do. Role model for them—show them your own creativity, enterprise, and passion. But also show them you can have fun and be kind to others, that you can weather disappointments and bounce back. Never lose the joy of parenting, the fraternity and friendship with your kids, or the belly laughs and silliness.

There is no question that potpourri parents love their children dearly and have their kids' best interests at heart. They devote so much of their time and energy toward enhancing their kids. Potpourri parents are fiercely competitive, applying for spots in the most prestigious preschools before their babies are even born. They will tell you how much they enjoy being parents, that they have fun watching their kids discover inner excellence, unmask hidden talents, and mature into successful young adults. But take a careful look at some of those parents at spelling bees, Little League tournaments, debate competitions, piano recitals, and swim meets. Do they *look* like they are having fun? More importantly, watch their kids. Do *they* look like they're having fun?

In an earlier chapter ("The Checkered History of Parenting Advice"), I promised not to delve too deeply into the myriad parenting philosophies that have come and gone and, in some cases, come back again. So here's the condensed version: find balance. Motivate your kids, but don't forget to giggle with them. Mix study time with downtime, goal setting with ice cream sundaes. As parents, we all share one important fact of life: our kids grow up too fast. It is true that if we don't push our kids hard enough, they may miss getting the inspiration, structure, and mentoring they need from us. But it is equally true that if we push too hard, our kids may miss being kids, we will miss the delight of watching them be kids, and we will lose the chance to be a bit of a kid ourselves when we're with them.

Find the balance so you'll have *no regrets* about how you spent the irreplaceable time you have with your kids.

And now, move on to Part 2 for the practical advice: How to find the time you need with your kids, and how to make the most of the time you find.

PART 2
No Regrets Parenting
Simple Strategies

Calendars

Their "Week at a Glance"

The truest measure of you as a person may be your calendar. Yes, the one that sits on your desk, beeps from your phone, or pops up on your tablet or computer monitor. The choices and commitments you make in your daily scheduling reflect the life you live and the priorities you set. If your calendar were to fall into the hands of a stranger, what would all the entries—the notations, meetings, phone calls, and appointments—say about you? Would the stranger reading your calendar recognize how important being a parent is in your life?

Calendars are all about time management. What better place to start managing your time with your kids than with your calendar? What better place to begin *No Regrets Parenting?*

Before you go to sleep each night, update your calendar with what's on tap for your kids tomorrow. Write it down, or type it in. Better yet, sit down with the kids and put their schedule for the whole week on your calendar every Sunday night. When they're young, your kids' schedules are usually more straightforward than yours: day care or school, perhaps followed by an after-school activity, dinner, homework, and bedtime. But as they get older, the choreography of kids' lives can get very, very complex. Make it a point to know where your kids are and what they're doing.

There are compelling reasons for putting your kids' schedules on your calendar. First, it's nice to know what's going on in your kids' lives. When you are in touch with their activities, you never lose touch with what is important to them. Your conversations with your kids at dinner, at bedtime, and in car pool are all more meaningful if you can talk with them about their day. Glance at your calendar before dinner tonight to remind yourself of what was on the kids' agenda today.

Second, there may be important activities in your kids' day that you should not miss. It's painful to find out about the class presentation or school assembly that you could have fit into your schedule if you had only known about it. Or that your little goalie blocked eight shots in a soccer game you only found out about after it was over. Of course, you still have to work (to afford to enroll your kids in soccer!), and it's very likely that you won't be able to get to all or even many of your kids' events—but if you don't know about them, you won't get to *any* of them. And you may get a pleasant surprise—one of your meetings that had conflicted with your child's after-school basketball game was canceled! Because the game is on your calendar, you're reminded that if you hurry, you can get there just in time to watch the second half.

Third, knowing where your kids are supposed to be throughout their day gives you an early warning system in case they're *not* where they're supposed to be. Keeping track of your kids' whereabouts is not spying or invading their privacy—it's good parenting.

Finally, and this is the punch line, your kids' daily activities should be your top priorities, and top priorities should be in your calendar. If there is a way to share those moments with them, by showing up at events where parents are invited (and when your kids will not be embarrassed!), that should be your first choice for how to spend your time. Their student council campaign speech, diving catch, perfect pirouette, three-point shot, or double axel will never happen again, at least not exactly the way it did today. Hearing about it afterward is bittersweet when you realize you could have been there.

There are no instant replays in real life.

Major Holidays

Christmas, Passover, birthdays, Thanksgiving, July 4th, Mother's Day, Father's Day, and the other Big Days of the year are the perfect occasions for parents to cement lifelong memories for their kids. With the built-in customs and culture of each holiday as a template, you should personalize each special day with your family's unique imprint. Establish traditions that your kids will look forward to for weeks before the holiday—a special food, a family skit or talent show, a dress-up dinner, decorations, touch football in the backyard, the movie you watch together every year on the same day, an arts and crafts afternoon, a fireworks show. And then, make sure you and your kids prepare for those rituals together—cooking, baking the cake, rehearsing, picking costumes, decorating, buying supplies.

As wonderful as they can be for bringing family together, major holidays can also be double-edged swords—oftentimes the Big Days involve lots of extended family and friends in the festivities. While it's nice to celebrate with others, make sure you set aside time just for your nuclear crew—a quiet breakfast, hot chocolate together before bed, a walk through the park. When your kids anticipate the upcoming holiday, they should think of the happy times they are going to spend with you, doing things together that all of you do only on that special day each year. And they should look forward to preparing for the rituals of each holiday that are unique to your family.

They will pass those traditions on to their own kids someday, and if you're lucky, they'll invite you to watch the reenactment, now through your eyes as grandparents. What a joy!

Half-Birthdays and Minor Holidays

There is special electricity in the household on holidays. Big Days in the life of the family—birthdays, anniversaries, Mother's Day, Father's Day, Thanksgiving, Christmas—create unique memories and establish lifelong traditions. So, why limit the excuses to celebrate together to a few days a year? You don't need to cook a turkey or give gifts for the kids' half-birthdays, but celebrating half-birthdays gets everyone together for cake and ice cream, or a special dinner or movie night, twice as often. And for that matter, why not a mini-celebration for quarter-birthdays? Besides having birthday fun *four* times a year, it will help your kids learn fractions!

Declare other family holidays. Observe the first day of school each fall, the last day of school each summer, a good report card, the last of the booster shots at the doctor's office, the first lost tooth, the last lost tooth, your dog's birthday, opening day of baseball season, closing day at the amusement park, the first snowstorm, the first crocus in the garden. Identify those days of the year that have special meaning for your kids and turn those days into events—not major events or major celebrations, nothing expensive or fancy, just events everyone looks forward to, jokes about, and shares together.

Momentous Moments

*Y*our kids' daily activities are hard to squeeze into your own calendar constraints, and you probably will have to miss many of them even if you know about them in advance and have entered them in your calendar. But there are certain events you should *never* miss, lest the years go even faster and in more of a blur than they already are. Truth is, especially when your kids are younger, they may not remember whether you were there for each of their "first" events and "big" events. But as you look back, the more of those you've been to, the more you'll feel a part of your child's life. And best of all, technology allows you to "be there" even if you can't actually *be there.*

Never miss the day your child takes her first steps, the first day of kindergarten, the first day riding a two-wheeler without training wheels, the first piano recital, the first day behind the wheel of a real car. Never miss the holiday pageant at school even if your child is just the bunny in the back. Never miss the fifth-grade continuation ceremony or the high school graduation, the first day of Little League or the first day on skis. His first ice skating performance in the big arena, or the first time she swims all the way across the pool.

How can you possibly be there for all of those momentous moments and still keep your job and fulfill your adult responsibilities? One word: video. Ask your spouse, your neighbor, your kids' babysitter, or classmates' parents to record, on their phones or tablets, the momentous moments you must miss. And then repay the favor to help others capture their kids' momentous moments.

So, when reality hits and you simply cannot get there, you and your little star can share the moment together afterward as she sits on your lap and narrates the big event for you as you watch it together on video. Not only does video capture the momentous moments you had to miss, but it also lets you send those moments to grandparents, replay them for family movie night, and embarrass her with them at her wedding reception.

Yes, her wedding reception. The years are short indeed, so capture as many of the momentous moments as you can.

Weekends

The premise and promise of *No Regrets Parenting* is turning scarce minutes into cherished moments, transforming everyday routines into opportunities for precious time with your kids. So, it may seem a little contradictory to make a big deal out of weekends. They are obviously designed perfectly for together time and shouldn't even need mention.

But weekends do need mention, as well as careful attention. In the new reality of two-working parent families and, increasingly, two jobs *per* parent, weekday responsibilities have crept into our weekends. Six- and even seven-day workweeks are not unusual. And although kids' weekends are still protected from school, your kids' programmed activities can quickly consume their weekends, too. Volleyball matches, swim meets, theater practice, baseball tournaments, Sunday school, birthday parties, and playdates—to say nothing of homework—bring Mondays back far too quickly. So quickly that between your responsibilities and the choreography of your kids' schedules, you may barely see your kids even on weekends. And remember, there are only 940 weekends between your baby's birth and her graduation from high school—how many have you already spent rushing past each other on the way to Monday?

For those reasons, all of the suggestions in the coming chapters for squeezing special time with your kids from the hectic weekday chaos—chauffeuring car pool, bedtime rituals, family dinners, pajama walks, sharing chores, family movie nights, etc.—apply equally well to hectic weekends.

Don't take weekend time for granted and don't assume that you and your kids will find one another without advanced planning. Synchronize your weekend calendar with your kids with the same rigor and vigor that you apply to coordinating your weekday calendars. There are many more options for family activities with a two-hour chunk of time on a weekend than with a half-hour slot on weekdays; plan ahead and be creative with those options.

Of course, if you and your kids are fortunate enough to have even bigger blocks of time available on weekends, reminiscent of a simpler time, take full advantage. Day trips to the state park, long bike rides, an outing to the amusement park, a college or professional sporting event, the museum, a day with the family on the golf course or at the lake, etc. The beauty of weekends, if you and your kids actually have time off, is that you don't have to *squeeze* activities into precious moments—you can *luxuriate* in activities that keep you together for several hours at a time. Your kids will feel the difference. The calm that comes with unhurried hours, versus the pressure that comes with scarce minutes, is rejuvenating and makes Monday more bearable.

Sleep

Pajama Walks

The hour before bedtime can be chaotic with young kids, one of several "witching hours" for young families. There is lots of advice out there, but little real science addressing the best ways to calm and quiet the kids before tucking them in. One of my favorite techniques, weather permitting, is a pre-bedtime pajama walk. Not only does it give kids gentle, tranquil moments to decompress from their hyper after-dinner activities, but it also gives parents special moments with their kids that otherwise might have been lost to TV.

The key to pajama walks is the pajamas. Get the kids completely ready for bed—teeth brushed, faces washed, pajamas on. Then put them in their stroller, or on their tricycle, or in their sneakers, and meander slowly around the neighborhood. No snacks en route (their teeth are already brushed!); don't kick the soccer ball along the way or bring the baseball mitts; postpone animated conversations until tomorrow, and *no phones or other devices*! These are the *mellow* moments.

It may take a couple laps, but by the time you arrive back home with your kids, they will be in a fresh-air trance and ready for bed; they may even fall asleep on the way and just need your tender transfer into the house and under the covers. One less witching hour for parents to deal with.

The "La-La Song"

Your kids are never more angelic, never more serene, and never cuddlier than in the moments just before they fall asleep. That is, of course, after you've survived the crescendo that builds right before bedtime, the protests about not being tired, the three glasses of water, and the last-minute homework panic.

Bedtime rituals give kids a sense of security and stability. When you are part of those rituals, your presence becomes fixed in your child's mind, associated with the tranquility and comfort of their bed and their good dreams. Establish a ritual, and be there to participate in it. It may be a pajama walk (see the previous chapter). It may be a lullaby, a story (see the next chapter), a chat about the day just passed, a prayer, or just a few minutes of holding each other. Our ritual was a bedtime story followed by the "La-La Song"; we replaced the words of an old folk song, popular before the kids were born, with La-La's. We La-La'ed the same tune every night, in a soft voice, while holding them or lying next to them. Soon the "La-La Song" became our family's comfort song; anytime of the day, whenever the kids were upset or frightened, we'd La-La them until the crisis passed.

There are seven nights in a week—plan to be there at bedtime for most of them, even if it means going back to the office some nights. When your kids get older, the rituals may change. Your adolescents may just want a kiss on the cheek as *you* go to bed because they are still doing homework. Or in the summer, it may just be a phone call to say goodnight because your teens are out later than *your* bedtime. But you should be part of every bedtime at every age.

Trust me—when they're away at college or on their own and their old beds at home are empty, you'll miss those bedtime traditions. Don't miss them when the kids are still home.

Story Time

There are so many good things to say about bedtime stories. From just a few months of age up until the "middle age" years—at least seven, eight, or nine—kids love stories almost as much as parents love reading or telling them. There are some books that we read hundreds (*hundreds!*) of times to our kids as they were growing up. We knew every word by heart. There were times when our kids had to remind us to turn the page because we were reciting the story from memory and our minds had wandered mid-paragraph.

Story time can be so much more than reading storybooks to your kids. Make up stories without a book. Use puppets (socks work just fine). If you can draw, illustrate the story as you're making it up. If you can sing, sing the story. Tell stories of your own life, funny and moving things that happened when you were a child, or what your parents taught you, and where they took you. Use story time to make your life before having kids a vibrant image in your kids' minds. How I met Daddy, how pretty Mommy looked when I saw her for the first time, what the army was like, your college roommate's funny habits, and the people in your dorm. Old yearbooks make great story-time material. Use your wedding album, or photo albums of your kids when they were babies or too young to remember their outings. Tell them about their adventures when they were little and how funny it was when they got scared by the raccoon at the campsite, when they got stuck at the top of the Ferris wheel, or when they sat on a horse for the first time. (Our oldest child never tired of the true story, with pictorial proof, of his first real horseback ride when everyone else got horses with macho names like Lightning, Thunder, Blaze, and Cannon, but he got Lumpy. He still laughs when we remind him!) Use a world atlas to tell your kids bedtime stories about faraway countries you've visited or read about, or how the oceans are all connected; show them where the Inuit and Yupik live.

Leave plenty of time before lights out for an unhurried, leisurely tale. Bedtime stories should never feel rushed, no matter how desperate you are to have some quiet adult time before your own bedtime—even if it means you have to stay up a little later yourself. You will be rewarded by having your kids start to request their favorite stories—"Tell the one about how Grandpa took you to the rodeo and you won a ribbon," or "Tell me about the night you first took Mommy to the movies," or "Tell me about the Inuit and Yupik again." How great is that!

Sleepless Sleepovers

I have never figured out what it is about sleepovers that kids love so much. Anyone of voting age knows that a night slept in your own bed is a guarantee of a better night's sleep than one spent anywhere else. Certainly, no right-minded adult would ever prefer to sleep at a friend's or relative's house unless it was at the bottom of a ski mountain or overlooking the ocean.

Yet, kids of all ages, even teenagers who should know better, still want to sleep at friends' houses. Probably has something to do with lax rules and late bedtimes. Very little actual sleeping occurs at sleepovers. Come to think of it, maybe it's best we don't exactly understand the appeal of sleepovers. But we should take advantage of them. Make your house the preferred sleepover destination. Serve the best snacks, stream the best movies, prepare the best pancake breakfasts. Having your kids' friends spend time at your house gives you a wonderful window into the relationships your kids have and into the lives of the friends your kids hang with. There's also the control feature—you're in charge of the movies they watch and the bedtime they keep. You make sure they brush their teeth and wash their face. You can peek in on the activity and eavesdrop on the conversations. You can even sneak a goodnight kiss when none of their friends is looking.

Although it's easier to ship the kids elsewhere than it is to host a houseful, the more time they sleep away, the less time you get to see them in their element, and the fewer goodnight kisses you get. And when your kids sleep elsewhere, some other kid's parents get to spy on your kids—who knows what your child may say to totally embarrass you!

But as hard as you try to win the "Sleepover House of the Year Award," you won't always get to be the host—your kids will want a turn elsewhere, and other parents are reading this book, too, vying for host honors. Although sending your kids to a friend's house for a sleepover does little to deepen your insight into your kids' lives, it's not all bad, either. Sleeping at a friend's house builds your child's self-confidence and independence; it prepares her for school trips, sleepaway camp, and, ultimately, her college dorm or first apartment. So don't feel guilty when your kids have a great time at an away sleepover; they will grow from the experience. Learn what made it fun for them, and steal the best ideas for your next sleepover event.

It's time to invest a few bucks and buy a comfortable air mattress or two for your new house guests. Maybe the other parents won't think of that!

While They Were Sleeping

*A*mong the most common complaints of parenthood is the diametrically opposite sleep habits kids have compared with adults. Very young kids go to bed early and wake early; older kids stay up much too late and sleep past noon. But, although frustrating at times (especially when toddlers are ready to roll at 6 a.m. and teens are just rolling in at midnight), the differences in sleep schedules between you and your kids present the perfect ploy for balancing your work hours with the hours you want to spend with your kids.

When your kids are young, schedule more work in the evenings after they've gone to bed; when your kids are older, use the early morning hours to work when they're still sleeping. Nap time, Mother Nature's glorious gift to parents of young children, presents additional opportunities for sneaking adult productivity into life with kids.

Of course, not all work time is flexible. Punch clocks and teleconferences can't be manipulated around bedtimes and nap times. But work that can be shifted should be—housework, take-home reading, email, internet research, and other tasks that spill over from your regular work schedules are prime candidates for creative rescheduling. As great a temptation as it is to take advantage of finally getting everyone to sleep for some well-deserved downtime for yourself, this is a chance to reprogram your idea of downtime into the concept of together time. If you can get some of your work done while they are asleep, you'll be able to spare more time from work when your kids are awake.

Of course, you still need downtime, away from the kids, to collect yourself and find balance (see "Staying Sane" in Part 1). Kids at all ages sleep a lot longer than you do, meaning you can squeeze in a couple hours of work and still have time for your own repose.

School

Homework Helper

This is a tricky one. You already went through second grade yourself; now it's your child's turn and you shouldn't be the one doing "times tables." But . . . you should *know* that your child is doing times tables, should look over her homework after it's finished every night, and should be there to help just in case 4 times 8 becomes 24. Homework checking time is a wonderful opportunity to sit close to your child, maybe while he's in pajamas and maybe with a cup of cocoa, and provide positive reinforcement for a job well done—or constructive advice on how to do it better tomorrow night. Homework helps kids build independence and learn to take responsibility, so don't feel that you have to compulsively check each math problem or spelling lesson for minor mistakes—that's not the point of homework helping. The point is that this is a valuable together time with your kids, and it shows them that homework matters to you and should matter to them.

Don't just ask, "Finished your homework?" and wait for the inevitable (and exasperated) "*Yessss*, Dad!" Make it a ritual to have your kids show you the finished product—not because you don't trust them, and not because you're worried about the dangling participle they may have missed, but because you are proud of the work they do and it makes you happy to see them doing such a nice job. Your pride in their work will become *their* pride in their own work.

How long should this ritual go on? Through middle school. By high school, your kids will have gotten all the right messages from you about homework and then will be ready for the autonomy that brings with it the nightly question from *outside* the closed bedroom door: "Finished your homework?" ("*Yessss*, Dad!")

High school doesn't mean you stop reinforcing the importance of homework; it just means you don't cuddle up every night and see the actual workbook pages. But stay in touch: ask your child how their homework grades are, and ask them to see the comments written by teachers on the graded homework. That gives you ongoing opportunities for praise and pride. And make sure your high schoolers know you are available to help with their homework if they *ask* for help. That assumes, of course, that by the time your kids are in high school you can still understand their schoolwork well enough to help.

Science Fair and "Super" Homework

Not all homework is equal. Some school assignments warrant more of your direct, hands-on help than others. Big projects—like those dreaded dioramas, nature-collection wall posters (butterflies, biomes, mushrooms, pinecones, seashells, etc.), life-size models of the solar system, and Popsicle-stick bridge-building contests. Even though your house looks like it may never recover from the assault of construction paper, superglue, and pine needles, and you are exhausted from the late-night runs to the hardware store or hobby shop, you should look forward to "super" homework assignments. They offer special moments of teamwork between you and your kids, with an important twist—in *this* collaboration, your child is the team leader and you are the assistant. If you forget that it's their project, you'll lose the uniqueness of the time together and you will send the wrong message about taking responsibility.

Preparing for science fair is a wonderful example of "super" homework together time. The moments you and your kids spend confirming the existence of gravity, determining the tensile strength of steel, assessing age and gender determinants of memory, or predicting the particle distribution of potential biological warfare agents can be priceless quality time together. Since it's unlikely that you are already an expert in any of those subjects, you and your child will learn together. You teach her how to research a subject, think about which questions to ask, and design a research plan to answer those questions.

Don't panic. Of course, the teachers at school will lay the foundation and establish the rules and guidelines to follow for the big project. But parental involvement is welcomed by most teachers, if for no other reason than to prevent the kids from burning down the house. For these "super" homework assignments, even though you've already been through middle school yourself (see the previous chapter), you get to work more closely and be more helpful than would be appropriate for nightly math or social studies homework.

Your kids need your help, their teachers encourage it, and you get meaningful and memorable time with your kids. Super!

Book Club

Teach your kids to love reading while involving yourself in *what* they're reading. Routinely ask them what they think about what they read. When your kids are assigned a book to read for school, you should read it, too. Or at least skim through it. At the same time, and at the same pace. Sometimes this may mean that you need two copies of the book (that's what libraries are for); usually you just pick up the book when your kids put it down to do other homework.

Though reading the book your child is reading for school isn't always a stimulating experience for you, it does give you valuable insight into their world. But don't stop there. Your kids should be reading books for pleasure, not just because of a school assignment. Here's another way to "double dip" (one of the "Staying Sane" strategies in Part 1 of this book) while parenting: when your kids are reading their fun books, you can be reading your fun books at the same time, in the same room, with the same bowl of popcorn or pot of hot apple cider. Reading defies age and avoids the tedium that sometimes comes with trying too hard to spend every minute with your kids doing kid activities. Seeing you read, like everything else your kids subconsciously study about you, tells kids that reading is important to you and should be important to them.

Reading skills correlate better than any other metric with success in college and beyond. When your kids are young and impressionable, teach them to love reading by reading with them. And then someday, maybe when they're in college or on their own, your kids may even recommend books for you to read because they enjoyed them and thought you might, as well.

Room Parents and School Volunteers

*F*ew adult volunteer activities are more productive, more necessary, and more welcome than those available at your kids' school. Every school, public and private, is underfunded and shorthanded. The school can use your help. Regularly spending part of a school day at your kids' school gives you an up-close look at what your kids see—their teachers and friends, hallway dynamics, and locker lore. For some, being a room parent is ideal—working closely with the teachers and other parents for school programs, fundraising, field trips, etc. For others, it may be volunteering in the office or lunchroom, hallway monitoring, or standing on the corner as a crossing guard. Drive for field trips, keep the scorebook at basketball or baseball games, chaperone class social events, be the "cast mom" for the school play or the assistant coach/helper dad for the track team. It's valuable to get to know your kids' schoolmates and the other parents. When you have experienced the context of their school lives, your dinner conversations and car-pool rides become more interesting and relevant for you and for your kids. You know their turf and even speak their language a little better. More importantly, you also gain a clearer understanding of your kids' worries and phobias, fallouts with friends, and playground gossip; these insights all pay dividends when your kids come to you for advice.

There's another benefit to volunteering at school. When you volunteer, the teachers and the principal know you are an involved and committed parent. Kids of involved and committed parents get a little extra attention, and parents get a slightly earlier warning if concerns arise about their kids. It should not be a calculated or planned benefit for parent volunteers, and certainly not one that is promoted or that teachers will even admit to, but when you're around the school more, the opportunities for interacting with your kids' teachers are increased, and everyone knows you are "watching." Ask most teachers what they most hope for at the start of every school year and they'll tell you—involved parents.

As there are special benefits, there is also a noteworthy downside to school volunteer work—it may absolutely mortify your kids for their friends to see you hanging around the school. When your kids are young, seeing you in the hallway is usually a thrill for them and they run to give you a hug. But as they get a little more socially aware, your presence becomes more chilling than thrilling. Be sensitive to your kids' feelings about this—if your being at the school embarrasses your kids, find a way to stay close but from a safe distance. Work on the school newsletter or help design the school web page from your home office, spend a few weekend hours at the school helping the teachers or administrative staff catch up on test grading or other paperwork, plan the sports banquet or teacher appreciation day, volunteer with the school's after-hours program for working parents.

That pit-in-your-stomach feeling about how fast your kids are growing up, the one you get each time your child finishes another year in school ("How in the world can third grade already be over?!"), will ease a little if you've shared a part of their school experience.

Back-to-School Nights
and Teacher Conferences

*D*on't miss any opportunities to hear about what's going on in school, and especially what's going on with your kids in their classroom. The more you know about school, the better able you are to share the learning experience with your kids. Early in the school year, back-to-school nights give you a chance to hear about changes in the curriculum, meet new teachers and staff, and tour the facilities. After some weeks or months, parent-teacher conferences put you and your kids' teachers face-to-face to discuss your kids' performance and progress in the classroom.

If you're reading this book, I don't have to convince you how important it is to keep your finger on the pulse of your kids' schoolwork. But, as with everything else in these chapters, back-to-school nights and parent-teacher conferences bring the added benefit of quality moments with your kids. Though it's true that kids typically don't accompany you to school for these events, the sharing begins when you get home. There are few things about school that kids enjoy (or fear!) more than hearing what their teachers said about them and what you think about their teachers. The time you spend with your kids "debriefing" after the parent-teacher conference is fun, gossipy, and very practical—you get to tell them what they are doing right and what they could be doing better at school, and they get a chance to respond. This all sets a great tone for your ongoing involvement in your kids' education. And kids learn even more from these discussions. They learn that teachers are human, can be approached and spoken to, and want kids to succeed.

Seeing that *you* are not intimidated by talking to teachers, and learning from you how to do so respectfully, establishes a template for your kids to feel comfortable discussing schoolwork with their teachers as partners in the learning process—a skill that will play well when they avail themselves of professors' office hours for help and advice in college or have performance evaluation meetings with their boss at work. Parents and teachers are typically the most important authority figures in a child's life. When those authority figures get together to talk about that child, it's big news that's worth sharing.

Occasionally a more dramatic intervention into your kids' parent-teacher relationships may be needed. If your child is struggling in a class or you suspect the dynamic between the teacher and your child is strained, you might consider scheduling a cameo appearance during actual class hours. Sitting in the back of the classroom can give you an unparalleled perspective for reconciling your child's version of events that you heard at dinner with the teacher's version that you heard at parent-teacher conferences or via a call from the principal. Your being in the room, during class, serves multiple purposes. You put your child on notice that this is the real deal, that you are taking a day off from work, and that you are even willing to risk potential embarrassment to your child to get to the bottom of the problem. You also show the *teacher* that this is the real deal—that you are engaged, an activist in your child's education. It puts both your child and her teacher on their best behavior, at least for the day, but often there is a carryover when both parties know you might be back. Avoid the temptation to automatically "side with" your child and blame the teacher. Though, in your child's eyes, that would make you his best friend, it isn't parenting. In most situations, the teacher has identified a real problem with your child's learning or behavior that needs to be solved, and you will have a better idea of how to solve it after your visit. But, importantly, there *are* times when the teacher's behavior may be the problem and, if so, your visit puts you in a much better position to seek a solution for that as well.

Parent–Teacher–Student Teamwork

*P*TAs, PTOs, and PTSOs are vital to a school's health. They do not, per se, increase the time you have with your kids; in fact, the meetings may take you away from home during homework hours or other family time. But . . . the long-term benefits of active membership in your school's parent-teacher group are substantial and include many of those associated with school volunteering and room parenting (see the earlier chapter). Knowing what's going on at school, showing the teachers that you are an involved parent, and keeping your ear to the ground regarding the school's direction are all invaluable for maximizing your child's classroom experience. The enrichment programs, extracurricular activities, and teacher support functions developed and implemented by parent-teacher organizations help to navigate the school toward shared goals. You will be a better partner in your kids' education when you invest your time in their school.

But that's not to say that your PTA/PTO/PTSO involvement should exclude your kids. On the contrary, it gives you a great opportunity to share an important experience with them. Tell your kids when you're going to meetings, and ask them for suggestions to bring to the other parents and to the teacher reps. What works in your kids' classrooms and what doesn't? What are the biggest problems with the cafeteria, the gym, the assemblies, or the field trips? Where should fundraising dollars be directed to have the most benefit for your kids' classes? Including your kids as advisers and allies in your organizational activities lets them know that you respect their opinions enough to ask and to act on them, and gives you yet another way to be your kids' advocate. It's like having your own personal "parent-student organization" at home, complete with its own meetings and refreshments.

College (and Career) Counseling

ollege isn't right for all kids, but the principles below are relevant for your high school students applying for any type of ongoing education as well as for those applying for their first real jobs.

Applying to college or for first jobs can be grueling and stressful for kids and their families. Most high schools offer college and career counseling services to their juniors and seniors; some parents hire private counselors to supplement what the school offers. College counselors help kids with everything from picking the most appropriate schools to apply to, writing personal statements (a.k.a. college essays), choosing which teachers to request recommendation letters from, practicing interview skills, and even deciding what to wear for interviews. Add to the college preparatory medley the standardized-test preparation centers and tutors who charge a hefty fee to help high schoolers improve their scores; the panoply of books with strategies for nailing your child's dream college that fill the bookstore shelves; and, of course, online counseling services aplenty. High school vocational counselors match students' competencies with the skills required for various jobs and career paths.

Why would you even consider leaving all this fun to others? But seriously, what's *wrong* with letting the professionals do all the advising and preparation of your kids for one of the most important milestones in their lives?

There are compelling reasons for you to be an important part of this process, not the least of which is the variable expertise and experience of college and career counselors. But there are two most important reasons.

First, if you have been practicing *No Regrets Parenting* since your kids were little, no one knows them as well as you do; and second, becoming intimately involved in your kids' application commotion can be the best quality time you will ever have with kids at this age. When you add the college or first "real job" application years (sixteen- and seventeen-year-olds) to the driver's ed years (fifteen- and sixteen-year-olds, with whom I will urge your active participation behind the wheel in a later chapter in this book), you can accomplish the near-impossible: salvaging many hours and days of quality time with your kids during their busiest and most exciting teen years, when the competition for their time is greatest. Having these experiences with your adolescents will set the stage for a true *no regrets* send-off after high school graduation.

College or job applications can be the most captive time you've had with your kids in one place since you moved their playpen into the kitchen seventeen years earlier (see the Epilogue—"My Favorite Letter"). Find a way to be an important part of this process. Your role may be as simple as taking your high schooler to your office with you on weekends and having her fill out applications while you catch up on work. Using your office as an application "war room" may help her better focus on the task at hand, with you close by for questions, advice, moral support, and lunch as needed. Or you may choose to become much more engaged in the process.

Pick those parts of the application process you feel most comfortable helping with. Maybe it's going online together to the websites of schools or companies she's interested in for virtual tours. Set up a chart together for comparing schools or other opportunities by characteristics that are important to her. Use the chart as you would a scavenger hunt list to negotiate each website—together, find the pieces of information you need to complete the chart, and pause along the way at other pages that look interesting for other reasons. Then use the chart to begin comparison shopping and narrowing down the choices.

College applications have three unique features not required for most job applications—standardized tests, personal statements (essays), and financial aid applications. Maybe you were good at standardized tests in your day and can help your son study for his. But even if you still get hives thinking about your own SAT, you can "proctor" his practice tests. Tell him when to begin and when it's "pencils down." When he's done with each practice section, go over the answers in the back of the book and help him understand the explanations given for each wrong answer. While he's in the middle of a timed forty-minute section, use that time for your own work or to catch up on emails—a rather sober but productive form of the "double dipping" strategy for staying sane as a parent that I described in Part 1 of the book.

Although many colleges are making standardized admission tests optional or eliminating them all together, that still leaves the dreaded personal statement or essay. Who knows your daughter's life experiences better than you? Brainstorm potential topics for her personal statement, and then help her with the final editing and proofreading. Of course, this must be *her* essay, but it's common for students to get a little guidance in choosing the topic and editing the final draft; professional college counselors and high school English teachers also help students with their essays.

Financial aid applications are a complicated but essential part of college applications. Often this job falls heavily on parents because they know where their tax forms are stored, but this is a wonderful opportunity to teach your kids the realities of budgets and bank accounts as they relate to tuition, books, room, and board. You can work on the financial aid bundle while she's writing her personal statement in the "war room" you've set up; then discuss both projects with each other.

Most colleges and job openings require letters of recommendation or references. Go over the pros and cons of potential letter writers and references together. If you've been practicing *No Regrets Parenting* all along, you know your child's teachers and outside contacts better than any college or career counselor could. Interviews are standard for all applications, college or job. Practice interviewing with your high schooler so they get comfortable hearing their own voice answering questions. The actual questions you practice are not as important as the play-acting that gets your child ready to face an interviewer without flustering.

Which colleges to apply to is a complex decision that will depend on your particular family dynamics (and on the success of your college-savings plan!). A somewhat simpler decision is which colleges to visit during the decision-making process. Whether he ultimately ends up at the community or technical college in town, the state university up north, or the Ivy League school thousands of miles away, a trip together to visit the schools that look especially promising is a memorable way to share this unique time in your kids' lives. Job applications are also opportunities for teamwork with your child in researching salaries and benefits, potential for advancement, quality of life issues, and work environment.

Finally comes the big decision about which college to attend or which job to accept. Now it's time for a family meeting (see the upcoming "Shareholder Meetings" chapter). Gather everyone together to debate the pros and cons of each option. Ultimately, of course, your applicant gets a bigger say than you or her siblings. It's your job to frame the discussion with adult perspectives on what's important to look for in a college or career, and on the financial realities. But everyone should weigh in on big decisions like this because they may profoundly affect the whole family.

Looking back, the process won't seem nearly as burdensome as you had feared. And you'll have the immense satisfaction that comes with sharing those precious moments on the eve of her leaving home. Oh my goodness! She's leaving home?!

Fear not. As you'll read in Parts 3 and 4, there's still a lot of parenting left even after they graduate from high school.

Work

A Corner (of Your) Office

*M*any of you don't work in offices, but whether your work is in an office, store, factory, warehouse, shipyard, or a spare bedroom in your home, sharing a bit of your workplace with your kids can be very rewarding for both you and your kids. In this chapter, I'll refer to your workplace as "office," but know these suggestions apply to wherever you work, including in your home.

First, a true confession. It can be a relief to go to work. When the frenetic energy at home reaches fever pitch, your office can be the perfect escape. Well, don't get too comfortable. Your office or other workplace can also be a special escape for your kids who need a change of venue for their big homework project, quiet reading assignment, or special milestone events—like studying for the SAT or filling out college and job applications (see the previous chapter).

Your office has distinct advantages over the library or a friend's house as a work refuge for your kids. First and foremost, you're there. By reserving a small corner of your workspace for your kids, you have found another way to share yourself with them. Your work is no longer a mystery, where you go each day is familiar, and your kids are included in part of your life they previously could picture only in their minds. Now when you talk about work at dinner, your kids know what you're talking about.

At your office, your kids know they have to lock in and focus on their own work—you're busy, others around you are busy, and there's no place for distractions. Their efficiency will be high and, hopefully, their presence won't reduce your efficiency—if that happens, they have to know you won't be able to bring them along again.

Finally, your office may be a place where you and your kids can work together. If it's their special project, you're close by for the occasional advice or guidance they may need. But they may also be able to help with your work. Really. Depending on your kids' ages, the work you give them to "help" you can just be pretend work to keep them occupied and near you. Draw a picture of Mommy working at her desk to show Grandpa; write as many words with more than two letters as you can for my file on big words; put all the big paper clips in this cup and the little ones in the other cup. But as they get older, your kids can be a real help with filing, data management, answering the phones, fixing the internet connection, etc. Your kids are probably better techies than you are—make them earn their keep. Real-world rules, however, may make bringing your kids to the office during work hours impractical—you don't want to irritate your coworkers or your boss. If you have access to your workplace off-hours or on weekends, use your work space as a retreat for quiet time with your kids when you or they have projects that spill over from the workweek. Usually you won't meet with objections to having kids with you when you're off the clock and the workplace is less crowded. Bring a special lunch or snack with you to make the visits more fun. Make sure you keep pictures of your kids on your desk or bulletin board; when they see their pictures, your kids know you think about them when you're at work and are proud to show them off to the people you work with.

Going to the office (or store, factory, warehouse, or shipyard) with Mom or Dad is a bigger deal for your kids than you might imagine—and taking them to work will change the way you look at your workplace even when they're not there with you. Who knows? It may even motivate you to clean the place up a bit!

Business Trips and Career Days

Sharing a corner of your workplace with your kids (see the previous chapter) is not the only way for them to understand what you do for a living and to learn about adult professions and careers.

If you travel for work, pick certain trips to take one of your kids along—but only *one* kid at a time. The experience of a one-parent-one-kid trip is very special for both you and your child, no matter how many kids you have. But if there is more than one child in your home, when else do you get to exclusively focus on, pamper, and take excursions with just *one* of them? Rotate trips among the kids so each knows that it's their turn the next time you can take a child with you.

The kid part of the trip can be almost free—they ride with you in the car or use your frequent flier mileage, and stay in your hotel room; they have to eat whether they are home or on the road with you. But, although not usually financially prohibitive, the logistics can be tricky. Successfully turning a routine business trip into an adventure for both you and your child requires thought and planning.

First, consider the business agenda for the trip; the more flexible your agenda, the better. How long is the trip? Ideally, it's long enough to allow for a couple nights in a hotel (as much as you may hate hotels, they are big fun for kids) and for at least a couple memorable excursions after each day's business is finished. What's the venue? Try to pick a business trip that takes you to a fun city. Big cities offer touristy things your kids will remember for a long time. Sure, Disney destinations are great, but visits to theme parks may require more time than a typical business trip allows and more money than your budget allows. But big cities offer lots of simpler expeditions that can be taken after each day's meetings: the elevator ride to the top of the famous skyscraper; a professional sports game; a bike ride across the famous bridge at sunset; or a dress-up theater production or concert. If your meeting locale doesn't offer pizzazz activities like those, find less famous, but still fun, local activities. Community theater, minor league baseball games, county fairs, miniature golf, and go-kart tracks also make for cherished moments and memories. No matter how high the skyscraper elevator climbs, how exciting the sporting event, or how fast the go-karts, it's being with you that your kids will remember most. And take plenty of selfies with your kids to refresh their memories as they get older.

Career days at school are like bringing a parent for show-and-tell. Your kids get to introduce you and be proud of what you do and of how interesting the other kids find you. But it's even more than that—career day can be the most effective way for *your* kids to understand what you do. Before your appearance in their classroom, rehearse with your child at home. Tell him what you plan to say and ask for advice on how to make it sound cool. Ask him if you should bring along visual aids—rocks if you're a geologist, model rockets if you're a rocket scientist, X-rays if you're a doctor, handcuffs if you're a police officer, a lasso if you're a cowboy. Think of hands-on ways to make your career come alive: Which rocks taste salty, which ones streak red on the sidewalk, and which ones flake and peel? How do the rocket components separate at each stage? Which bone is connected to the head bone? How tight are handcuffs? Who can throw a rope around the teacher? Don't worry if your career isn't as flashy as other parents'. Work with your child to explain how important what you do is—even if the other kids in class aren't dazzled by tax preparation, real estate sales, or bankruptcy law, your own child will have a better appreciation for the contribution you make. The best part of career day is the time you spend with your kids rehearsing your presentation and then talking about it afterward that night at dinner.

Take advantage of any opportunities for your kids to experience part of the life you lead while they're in school. Let them sit in the back row of lectures or presentations you are giving. Include them for company picnics and office outings; sign up for "take your daughter to work day"; bring them to your factory cafeteria for lunch. These are *No Regrets Parenting* moments, quality time that gives your kids a better understanding of who you are.

And a better understanding of where their allowance comes from (see the next chapter).

Making Lemonade—
Their Office (and Allowances)

Kids should start several businesses during their childhood, and teaching them how is a marvelous way for you and your kids to spend time together. It's also a great way to teach them about money, budgets, marketing, public relations, and working with others.

Start with the lemonade stand. My own childhood lemonade business taught me how to address adults as "ma'am" and "sir." It also resulted in my adulthood vow to never drive past a lemonade stand without stopping to buy. I always pay with a dollar bill to see if the kids can make change—and then I give them the change as a tip. Before setting your kids up at the lemonade stand, practice making change with them. Explain overhead and profit. Set a goal for the money your kids will make: teach them about savings and investments, shop ahead for the special purchase they can make when they've earned enough, or identify the charity to which your kids can contribute the earnings. Best idea—do all three. Teach your kids that there are many demands on income and that skillful budgeting can help meet all of those demands—for saving, investing, buying, and giving.

Lemonade stands should grow into more sophisticated businesses as your kids grow: lawn mowing, snow shoveling, gardening, babysitting, running a summer "camp" in your backyard for younger kids in the neighborhood. And when they're in their teens, you and they might enjoy starting an Etsy or eBay store together. The best part of all of these entrepreneurial ventures that you help your kids undertake is that *you* are helping your kids undertake them. You are strategizing with them, giving them on-the-job training, sharing their experience, teaching them life lessons, and watching them grow into junior citizens. And then you get to go to the bank with them, follow the stock market with them, shop with them, and learn with them about the charities they are supporting.

And it all starts with just lemons, water, and a little sugar.

Allowances can achieve many, but not all, the same goals with your kids as their lemonade stand. There are books written about using allowances to teach kids financial responsibility and generosity, and allowances do just that. Experts are divided on whether allowances should be tied to chores or given outright; most believe chores should not have to be rewarded and are just part of being in a family.

Allowances and lemonade stands are not mutually exclusive—both teach children important lessons and allow them to move on to bigger and better experiences with money.

Handymen, Handywomen, Handy Kids

Never fix a leaky faucet, change a tire, check the oil in the car, paint the fence, or replace the furnace filter while your kids are on Instagram or TikTok, playing video games, or watching TV. Turn off the device or TV and turn on the flashlight. You are your kids' source of knowledge for all things handy and practical. Arm them with the flashlight and talk to them all the way through the repairs you're making and the maintenance you're performing. Home improvements are a great way to spend time with your kids while teaching them about tools and life at the same time. The attic, the basement, and the crawl space are all classrooms for learning and opportunities for sharing. With the youngest kids, take advantage of their natural "I can do it" and "I do it myself" stage of development. Asking to take charge of a project that is far beyond their abilities at a young age is their way of growing self-confidence and prepares them to help with they're older.

As they get older, take advantage of kids' inexplicable love of ladders to coach them in caution and to build trust. For all but the oldest of your helpers, power tools are off limits, of course—but even those weapons of mass construction can be fun for kids, giving them a chance to wear goggles and ear plugs at a safe distance while you power up. Please pardon our dust.

Now that you've groomed your kids to help with projects, and when they're old enough to really contribute, *you* should start holding the flashlight for *them*, instructing them on how things work and how to safely fix things that don't work. New tile or countertops, built-in shelves, and paint jobs are bonus chances for time with your kids.

Whatever their ages, take them to the hardware store with you before the job begins, and then to the ice cream store when the job is finished.

Home

Kitchen (and Laundry) Duty

*I*t is often said that the kitchen is the focal point of the house. It can also be a focal point for time with your kids, even your youngest kids (see the Epilogue—"My Favorite Letter"). As tempting as it may be to put them in front of the TV while you're cooking dinner or cleaning up after meals, avoid that temptation. There's a lot for kids to do in the kitchen, and lots for them to learn. Start by letting them be the official tasters, and work up to water-glass fillers and table setters. All kids can benefit by being kitchen savvy, and even if it takes a little longer to get dinner on or off the table with all the "help" you're getting from the kids, it's worth it. Not only will your kids learn about healthy food choices, following recipes, cooking, baking, and table setting, but they'll also have bragging rights at dinner when everyone says how delicious the meal is. Even more important than the skills they'll pick up, the kitchen gives you unscripted and unprogrammed time for conversation and sharing. And your kids will have spent important moments with you as a role model, caring and providing for your family.

When the meal is done, your kids are the clean-up crew—again, avoid the temptation to send them away in the name of efficiency. Clean-ups are never as leisurely or interactive as meal preparation, but they do imbue your kids with a sense of nightly responsibility and teamwork. When you let kids run from the table after dinner, you are sending the message that it's your job to serve them, rather than the message that chores are a shared family responsibility. The wrong message here can lead to a sense of entitlement in other aspects of your relationship with your kids. Kids are entitled to your love, your protection, and your mentoring—they are not entitled to your bussing tables, dishwashing, and floor sweeping.

Although no one ever says the laundry room is the focal point of the house, many of the same togetherness benefits accrue while loading the washer, emptying the dryer, folding the clean clothes, and, when your kids are old enough, ironing. The messages to your kids are the same as those from kitchen duty: shared responsibility, no entitlements.

Come into My "Office"

Back in the '60s, there was a popular TV comedy show (more recently remade as a movie) called *Get Smart* about a bumbling but self-assured, and quite lucky, spy who worked for the good guys, an agency named CONTROL. The bad guys spied for KAOS, an evil international organization. Long before anyone had cell phones, our hero, Maxwell Smart, had a "shoe phone" (I guess today they would have called it a "Smart phone." Sorry about that, Chief!) and a "laser blazer" (laser beams that shot out from his sports coat button). Among the best devices of the show, though, was the "cone of silence," a plastic sheath that enveloped two people who needed ultimate privacy for important secret-agent business. No one outside the cone could hear the important talk going on inside. Predictably, in each episode, the cone helped CONTROL prevail over KAOS.

There should be a special place in every home, no matter how large or small your home may be, where heart-to-heart discussions are held in a "cone of silence" and control prevails over chaos. It may be an overstuffed love seat in the family room, a nook in the basement, a corner of the attic, or even the rooftop of your apartment building. When your kids have a crisis, real or imagined, say to them, "Come into my 'office' and let's talk about it." It may actually even *be* your home office where the tête-à-têtes take place—just make sure you're not sitting behind your desk with your child on the other side.

The point of designating an "office" for important home conversations with your kids is that it's a trusted and safe spot where they can bare their souls in private, and where you can patiently listen. This is the place where crises earlier in the day can be deferred to and dealt with (see "3D Parenting" in Part 1). This is where you can advise or sympathize, or bare your own soul. This special "office" space should be small enough for one-on-ones, and distinct from where the *whole* family gathers for the important "shareholder meetings" I describe in a later chapter.

There's a particular magic for a child knowing that he has your undivided, undistracted attention during times of worry or stress. No one else can enter or interrupt during these "office hours." The meetings often don't last very long, but they almost always end up with a plan, a kiss, and everyone feeling better than they did before the meeting started.

Control prevailing over chaos.

Grease Monkeys and Yard Hands

The garage is the most important part of your home that's not actually in your home. Whatever project you are working on in the garage can include your kids—from fixing the car, to tinkering with the lawnmower, to carpentry at your workbench, to sweeping out the mud that came in on the tires. Garages are laboratories, lecture halls, and libraries in your kids' life-skills education; garages are also unhurried venues for one-on-one time with your kids. Think how much more valuable it is for your kids to see you fix an old toy than it is to give them a new toy when the old one breaks—and think about all the different things you can talk about while doing the repairs. Garages hold vital values for kids—self-confidence, self-reliance, inquisitiveness, creativity.

The yard is another learning center for kids. Teach them about plants and flowers, and about saving water. Pull the weeds up by the roots, rake the leaves into a pile big enough to be a trampoline, and clean the gutters before the next rain. Clear the snow off the driveway with two shovels, one large and one small. Most importantly, listen to your kids' observations, answer their questions, and occasionally sprinkle them with the hose or hit them with a snowball just to keep it silly. At first your kids might prefer video games, social media, or YouTube to working outdoors, but they'll soon learn from you that heavy leaves in the bag and wet snow on the shovel are the best "downloads" of all. And, if you must, post videos of their leaf-jumping on Instagram or TikTok for them to share with their friends.

The Parent Pet Trap

*P*ets are such an obvious source of quality time and teaching moments with kids that it seems superfluous to write about all the benefits. From goldfish to gerbils, cats to canaries, and hamsters to horses, the menagerie of pet possibilities is endless. Every moment you spend teaching your kids how to care for animals is magnified many-fold by the larger life lessons you also teach: compassion, responsibility, selflessness, benevolence, humaneness. Pets can help kids grow their independence, and pets complete a triangle of companionship and love between you and your kids—each has a unique but interconnected relationship with the other.

Sounds idyllic, eh? But . . . I'm sure you can guess what I'm going to say next.

At the risk of sounding like the Grinch who stole Fido, here's a cautionary note: Remember that *No Regrets Parenting* is about finding quality time for special moments with your *kids*; it is *not* about spending time *alone* with "their" pets. Your days are hectic enough trying to fulfill adult responsibilities and salvage scarce minutes with your kids. Insofar as pets help you do the latter, terrific. But unless your kids are there with you to scrub the aquarium, change the litter box, fill the water bowl, clean the hutch, and throw the ball to the dog (even in a blizzard), I recommend you go to the zoo when your kids have a craving for a furry friend. If your kids aren't part of the triangle, pets become a parent trap. They take up precious time you could be spending more wisely with your kids. Ignore your kids' promises about taking full responsibility for the new pet they are pleading for; once the puppy settles in and the novelty wears off, they'll forget every vow they made. If your kids talk the talk, they have to walk the walk. And they have to walk the dog. Even in a blizzard.

The only way to protect yourself from the parent pet trap is with a contract. Contracts may seem a bit harsh when dealing with a five- or six-year-old, but they can be an important life lesson in and of themselves. A commitment is a commitment, and a contract formalizes a commitment. The contract needn't be written, although I prefer written agreements where pets are concerned—you can hang the contract on the cage or kennel and point to it whenever your kids forget whose pet it is and let the water bowl run dry. It can be as short as a line or two: "I promise that if my parents get a rabbit for me, I will feed and water my rabbit and help clean the hutch. If I don't, I know my parents may have to take my rabbit back to the animal shelter. Where it may get eaten by a Doberman." Okay, okay, you can leave out the last sentence. But you get the point.

You supervise, but the pet "belongs" to your child. The time you spend supervising is wonderful quality time—even the walks in the blizzard. But don't get caught out in the cold alone with your kids' pet.

Food

The Daily Dinner Meeting

Breakfast may be the "most important meal of the day," but dinner is the most important meeting in the life of most families (see next page* for an important disclaimer). At breakfast, everyone's in a rush to get where they have to be that day. Lunch? Fuggetaboutit. Nobody's home at the same time in the middle of the day. But dinnertime is the one recurring interlude in the day's disarray when the whole family may be able to coordinate their calendars and gather together. Everyone's hungry, everyone's pausing between the frenzy of the afternoon and the sometimes equally frenzied evenings, and everyone's tired and ready to sit down for a few minutes. When else do adults and kids have their biorhythms so synchronized?

By dinnertime, everyone in the household has accumulated a whole day's events to share with one another. There's good news and bad news, big developments and little developments. Every dinner is an opportunity to follow up on the discussions at dinner the night before. Look forward to dinner as a chance to reconnect with the people most important to you. Take turns telling the day's stories. As I dragged myself in the door after work, our kids would sometimes shout, "Wait till you hear what I have to say at dinner tonight!" What a wondrous thing to hear from a child.

It may start out slowly—come to dinner prepared with specific questions, because kids need prompting. When you ask, "So, what happened today?" they will typically answer "Nothing," or "Not much." "How was your day?" "Good." Don't settle for that. Prepare for your daily dinner meeting at home the way you prepare for your meetings at work—armed with an agenda of items you want to learn from your kids, and with news of your own day to share. Use what you talked about last night to start tonight's dinner conversation: "Did your English teacher give back your essay?" "Did your friends get in trouble for gluing the stapler to the desk?" "What did Enid decide about going to camp this summer?" "How did the tryouts go?" Show your kids that you remember what's going on in their lives and that you're interested. Here's a confession: I've even been known (only to myself, because I've never told this to anyone before) to make notes during the day about what I wanted to ask the kids at dinner, just to make sure I didn't forget and let a whole day go by without hearing the latest update. No, I didn't bring the notes to dinner ... but I did secretly sneak a peek at them before going to the table.

Be there for dinner. Put it on your calendar (at least your mental calendar) every day: "Dinner meeting with family." Even if you have to go back to work afterward, be there to share the day's events with your kids—theirs and yours. Insist that everyone be at dinner every night. You're allowed to make rules—you're the parent! Dinner together is one of the most important rules you'll ever make—and may be one of the hardest for you yourself to follow. But it's worth it. While you're making rules, make one more: no phone calls, text messages, or other interruptions during dinner (except emergencies, of course).

Soon you'll find yourself addicted to family dinners and upset on the very rare nights that unavoidable conflicts arise.

That's the whole point of a meeting.*

---

* Important disclaimer: As with all the suggestions in this book, remember that one size does not fit all. Every family is different, and every strategy must be tailored to your own unique situation. In some households, for example, coordinating dinner schedules may be impossible: Dad works late most nights, Mom has dinner meetings, kids have early-evening school activities; no one has time to slow down long enough to find each other for dinner. If that's your household, choose breakfast as your "must-meet meal." If everyone has an early morning, and even though everybody is rushed, make time for short breakfast meetings. Adjust the meeting "agenda" to the meal you choose: at breakfast, talk about the day before, or the day ahead, or plans for the weekend. Just be sure to talk.

After-School Attention (with Snacks)

This is very different from after-school *detention*. As your kids get older, the closing bell at school simply signals the beginning of more time commitments and programmed activities for them. Playdates, clubs, and sports quickly fill the few hours between the end of school and dinner. Make no mistake, these are critically important activities for your kids' growth and for your sanity. For many parents, after-school hours are still the middle of the workday, and knowing that your kids are engaged in safe and healthy activities provides peace of mind and fulfills a practical necessity.

But when your kids are still young enough to have half-day preschool or to come straight home after school, and on the days, rare as they may be, that you can be there to welcome them, a golden window into their day opens for you. The kitchen table or the sofa in the family room becomes a debriefing center, a venue for your undivided attention to your child, complete with milk and cookies or fruit and crackers. When it's warm, sit on the porch, or pack snacks and stop at a park on the way home. This is downtime when you get the chance to hear about their day while their memories are still fresh on the subject. As with dinnertime (see the previous chapter), don't accept "good" as an answer to "How was your day?" or "nothing" to "What's new in school?" Ask the right questions so you get multi-word responses, and withhold the cookies until you do. Tell them about your day, too, so you can earn a cookie.

After-school attention moments are often brief because real life comes calling—your work, their homework, errands, and dinner preparation. But brief is okay, because it's not long until dinner, when you will have the time you need to finish the conversations you started.

Tomorrow's Lunch Tonight

*I*t's rare that families can eat lunch together—we're all too scattered during the day. That's why I stressed how important the daily dinner meeting is a couple chapters back. But there is a way to "share" lunch and to squeeze in a few more minutes together before bedtime. With homework done and pajamas on, gather the clan in the kitchen to make tomorrow's lunch. Rather than pulling together all the lunches by yourself, help each other fill the lunch boxes or sacks that everyone will grab in their rush out the door tomorrow morning. Not only does this make it more likely that the kids will like what they find in their lunch, but it also decompresses the morning flail just a bit. While you and your kids are pillaging the fridge and the pantry, teach them healthy food choices, listen to a kids' audiobook, dance to music you and your kids both like ("Alexa, play 'Better When I'm Dancin'' by Meghan Trainor"), gossip a little, and talk about what's happening in their day tomorrow. While you're at it, nibble a bedtime snack or finish the dinner dishes together.

Then, after the kids have gone to bed, slip a little surprise into the lunch box they just packed, like a note that says, "I love you," a funny sticker of their favorite movie or TV character, or maybe something a little *un*healthy, like a chocolate Kiss.

The Corner Diner

A friendly neighborhood restaurant can become a wonderful excuse for spending, and extending, special dinnertime moments with your kids. Kids are creatures of habit (as, for that matter, are grown-ups). Kids don't need variety or diversity in their eateries—they probably even order the same item off the menu each time they go to their favorite place. Just the announcement that "we're going to the Corner Diner" can awaken the tired and taciturn souls that your kids often become by dinnertime. Use the restaurant to celebrate special events or to perk up a difficult week. Walk to the restaurant if you're close enough (that's why I named it the Corner Diner!)—that gives you even more time to talk.

Your special family restaurant doesn't have to be fancy or expensive; in fact, the more casual and laid-back, the better. The less the food costs, the more often you can enjoy the place; the healthier the fare, the better you'll feel about taking your kids there. It's not the gourmet ambience that gets your kids excited when you go out to eat; it's the simple enjoyment of going someplace special. Favorite foods on the menu stimulate the "pleasure centers" and flip on the "fun buttons" in your kids' brains (see "Brain Buttons" in Part 1), which increases their focus and their participation in the event. Sharing time with your kids while their brains and bellies are happy and satisfied makes you a part of that happiness and satisfaction.

It may sound heretical, in this day of a childhood obesity crisis, to link food with good feelings and good times. But the happy times your kids spend with you at the Corner Diner will not make them fat. What makes them fat is sitting in front of the TV or computer for hours at a time without you, eating junk food and not running around.

What about takeout, the drive-through, and fast-food places? Each may have its place in your family dynamic, and the speed and convenience of those venues can be attractive and fun. But the extra time you spend sitting down together at the Corner Diner—waiting for the waiter to fill your order, for the water glasses to be refilled, and for the check to finally arrive—gives you moments with your kids that are lost at home to the pull of the TV, cell phones, video games, social media, and even the backyard. Kids are captive in a sit-down restaurant—nowhere to run, nowhere to hide. It's intimate time, knees touching in the tiny booth, sharing the news of the day.

And for bringing all of you these cherished moments together, give your compliments to the chef and a nice tip to the patient waitperson who has to clean up the mess your kids just made.

Taco Night

*D*inner at home with the whole family is special unto itself, but there are easy ways to make it even more special. Taco night, pizza night, Chinese-food night, egg night, pancake night. You already know that kids love to go out to eat, and they're often more animated and engaged in a restaurant than they are at home (see the previous chapter). But you don't need to go to restaurants to experience fun venues and exotic menus. Turn your kitchen into a Japanese sushi bar or an Italian bistro once a week—or do each on a different night for twice the weekly benefit. Your kids will be even more excited about sitting down together if they have their favorite foods on a regular basis. And when kids are excited and having fun, they are energized in their conversation and in sharing their news at the dinner table.

Special dinner nights are also unique opportunities to increase your kids' involvement in the meal making, and thereby increase the quality time you spend with them. When there are recurring themes for dinner, kids can assume bigger roles in getting the food to the table, because they'll start to remember the routine from the last taco night: washing the vegetables, stacking the tortillas, mixing the salsa, grating the cheese, and gossiping about the latest news from school. You're still in charge of blending the margaritas! What a nice cantina you've created.

When the kids leave for school in the morning, remind them: "Taco night tonight!" They'll look forward to it all day.

Ice Cream Sundaes, Hot Cocoa, and Popcorn

Yes, there is a childhood obesity crisis in this country, and we certainly don't want to teach our kids that food brings comfort or that eating means security—reinforcing the physical and psychological joys of food is not a healthy parenting strategy. But, c'mon! Kids have to be kids, and when kids grow up to become adults and parents (I'm talking about you!), they still need to occasionally feel like kids.

Establish special traditions around fun treats—they become more special because they don't happen often. Hot summer Sunday afternoon sundaes, or cold winter family TV nights with hot cocoa, or full-moon parties with moon-shaped cookies, or popcorn balls on the day of the big game. Sprinkles make ice cream special, cuddling goes great with cocoa, black and white icing dresses up cookies, and popcorn is almost healthy for your kids. Now, please don't go around telling people that a pediatrician told you to feed your kids ice cream sundaes with sprinkles; I do have a professional reputation to maintain. So, for the official record, baked apples with cinnamon and raisins, angel food strawberry shortcake, snow cones made with apple juice, and banana splits with fat-free frozen yogurt work just as well and with less guilt.

The food is not the point—it just helps make the point. Fun foods and special treats are conversation starters and memory makers; they help imprint images of the great moments you spend with your kids in their minds, and push the focus buttons in their brains that you read about in Part 1. Your kids may not remember all the discussion topics or the jokes or the tickling, but they'll forever fondly recall the chocolate syrup and the marshmallows. Or baked apples and raisins. ☺.

And, of course, they'll remember the occasions that merited the special treats. And that they shared them with you.

Food Fights

*J*ust kidding. Bad idea. Move on to the next section.

Getting There

The Fly on the Dashboard

Y ou need to get to work, and your kids need to get to school. Perfect. Every morning presents a new opportunity to spend a few bonus minutes together. Even if you're heading in opposite directions, arrange your daily start time so you can drive car pool. Many schools even have an earlier drop-off option for working parents. Yes, your kids are still half asleep, you are already girding yourself for the upcoming hassles at work, there may be other kids in the car, and traffic is a nuisance.

But driving car pool tunes you in to each upcoming day in your kids' lives. Do they have gym today or study hall? Did they remember to bring their homework? Do they need a signed note for the field trip—and where is the field trip going, anyway? Is there a student assembly today? What's going on after school? Is that kid still being a nuisance at recess? What tests do they have today? Whoops! Better practice their spelling words on the way, too!

Car pool also lets you eavesdrop on real-time conversations between your kids and their friends. It is one of the well-known truisms of parenting that the driver of a car full of kids becomes invisible to the kids in the car—they act and talk and laugh and confide in each other as if the car were driving itself. Driving car pool is like being the proverbial "fly on the wall" during a few moments of your kids' social lives. It gives you a chance to hear how your kids relate to their friends, learn what kind of people your kids' friends really are, and get the scoop on what's important to your kids and their friends at these very random moments in their lives. What could be better than that?

Kids coming home after school are more animated (and more awake) than they are in morning car pool. If you can drive car pool home from school, you'll hear them talk about their day and about the homework they have to do that night. (I can't count how many times I learned about a project assigned last week—and due *tomorrow!*—from the conversation in the backseat on the way home from school.) You'll catch up on who said what to whom, and about who has a crush on whom. And all of this occurs without the kids ever noticing that you're there—the invisible chauffeur.

H. G. Wells, roll over!

School Bus Magic

*I*f you don't have the privilege (☺; see the previous chapter) of driving car pool because it's another parent's turn to drive or your kids take the bus, spend a few minutes with them at the curb each morning before their ride gets there. These can be magical together moments otherwise lost in the name of expediency, or drowned out by the cacophony of "music" blasting from your kids' earbuds.

The few minutes of your morning that you give up by waiting for your child's ride help you bring the day into focus, for both you and your kids. Ask them about what's going on at school today; tell them what you'll be doing at work; remind them about volleyball practice after school; quiz them on their geography facts for today's test; finish a conversation you started at the dinner table the night before; tease them about the special surprise dinner you have planned for tonight. When you add up all the bonus minutes you spend with your kids before the bus or car pool arrives, it amounts to more than *fifteen hours* each year if you're at the curb for just *five minutes* each school morning (*thirty hours* each year if the bus is running late!). That's time you'll never get back if you don't take advantage of it now.

And when the bus or car pool arrives, give them a big hug and tell them you can't wait to see them after school. Or, depending on their ages, sneak away before they have time to be mortified at the possibility of the other kids on the bus or in the car spotting you.

Road Trip

The best vacations are those that give you and your kids the most time together, without distractions and without interruptions. For any of you who have driven even short distances with young kids, this may seem like insane advice, but road trips can be the best family vacations of all. The time in the car, especially when your kids are "middle aged" (five to twelve years), is priceless "captive audience" time.

Making the most of road trips takes some creativity and planning. Stop at weird roadside attractions, eat at funky diners along the way, have family debates, play highway games that everyone in the car can play together (license-plate poker, I Spy, mileage math, states and their capitals, Twenty Questions). Have contests to see who can sing the words to the most songs on the radio (tip: you'll have to find an oldies station to give yourself a chance in that competition).

Most Important Road Trip Rule: No devices allowed that isolate you or your kids from each other. This is tough, because the earbuds for their cell phones and digital devices can be so tightly attached to your kids' heads that you may have considered surgical removal. You'll undoubtedly have to learn to live with connectivity conflict again when you get back home—but on the road, when you've got the kids to yourselves, keep them to yourselves.

When you make the road trip an adventure, the destination is even less important than the getting there and the getting back. Compare that with flying to a crowded theme park where there's little chance for everyone to talk to each other on the airplane (though I suppose the long security lines at the airport *could* be viewed as "together time"), and when you get there, the theme park attractions are really *distractions* from the time you can spend with the kids. Or compare a road trip to flying to the "family-friendly resort" where, again, there's no face time on the airplane, and the resort is loaded with kids' activities that separate you from them for most of the trip. I know, I know, kids-only activities sound like a great idea—you'd like a little adult time on vacation, too. Understandable. So, if you're going to a theme park or family-friendly resort, at the very minimum make sure everyone sits down to dinner together every night, and try to schedule at least some daytime activities that you all do together. If you have enough vacation days, *drive* to the resort or theme park to lessen the impact of the distractions and separation once you arrive. That way, by the time you get there, you've already had real time together, and on the drive home, you get a chance for a family recap.

If the biggest benefit of road trips is the up-close and personal time in the car, van, or RV, the next biggest benefit of a driving vacation is the lower cost compared to flying. Remember my promise in the "Money" chapter in Part 1 that the best times with your kids can be those that are free or inexpensive. Money for vacations is almost always tight, and even long road trips can be pricey when you factor in gas, motels, and food along the way—but they rarely add up to airfare for an entire family plus the rental car, and the hassle factor is so much less than at the airport and the rental car agency. There are ways of cutting road trip costs as well: camp out, pack food from home, and visit state parks and attractions that are closer and cheaper to get to. Your kids will remember vacations by how much fun they have, not by how exotic or expensive the trip was.

Vacation Bribery

When your kids are young, they go where you go for vacation. That's a real blessing, because as they get older, it's harder and harder to interest your kids in family vacations. They may already be in college or have summer jobs, busy social lives, and even invitations to join their friends on vacations. This is where you need to be especially creative. If you can afford "exotic" trips—Hawaii, Alaska, the Caribbean, Europe—that's great; even the busiest older kids, and the ones usually too cool to want a vacation with their parents, will bite on the exotic temptation. But for most, the extravagant vacation bribe is a rare or impossible luxury, so we need to tone down the bait without decreasing its effectiveness in getting the older kids on board.

Tailor the vacation to your kids' passions. Are they baseball fanatics? Drive to spring training in Arizona or Florida and buy the cheap seats on the outfield grass. Football? Go to their favorite team's August training camp where you can watch practices for free. Addicted to a special TV show? Write for free tickets to sit in the studio audience and plan your trip around the show. Movie lovers? Tour one of the big film studios. Chocoholics or candy addicts? The Hershey factory in Pennsylvania or the Jelly Belly factory in California; dozens of other confectioners are only a short drive from wherever you live. There are factory tours to suit every interest and in virtually every locale. Crayon, soft drink, automobile, motorcycle, greeting card, computer, RV, and cheese factories are scattered all over the country, and almost all offer tours. Plan your trip around a dog show, music festival, horse race, NASCAR event, outdoor art show, or hot-air balloon festival. Tour Elvis's home or Opryland or the CNN studios. Museums usually make kids yawn, but some museums are cool— science fiction, rock music, comic books, computers, outer space, race cars, trains, ships, movies, and spies all have their own museums. There are also Hall of Fame museums for almost every taste in sports and culture. Tourist traps work because they exploit people's passions and satisfy their curiosities. Passion and curiosity are the same traits you should exploit in getting your kids excited about the family vacation.

Do you love camping and hiking, but your kids are bored outdoors? Dial up the excitement factor with a canoe or kayak trip, rock climbing, spelunking, ice fishing, paintball, cross-country skiing, hut tripping, horseback riding, paragliding, or windsurfing. Make sure you factor in the cost of lessons so you don't have to factor in the cost of an emergency room visit.

Let your kids help plan the trip, and let them tell you what would make it more special for them. They may want to bring a friend—it's better to have your kids' friends on your vacation than to have your kids desert you for their friends' vacations. (Prepare yourself for the day your kids ask to bring a boyfriend or girlfriend along. I'll leave it to you to handle that one, except to confide that we said "yes.")

Admit it. Bribery is a big part of parenting at all ages, anyway. Why shouldn't it be a part of family vacation planning when your kids are old enough to have vacation ideas of their own?

Unplugged

Next time you're at a stoplight, take a peek inside the minivan stopped next to you. The driver (parent) is talking on the phone; the kids (they're the ones with the white earbuds) are listening to "music," texting, or watching the dropdown TV screen in the backseat; and the family dog is staring at you through the partially open back window, desperate for someone to notice him. Only the dog is unplugged and fully aware of his surroundings. Each human is entranced in a personal digital space, separated from one another not by physical distance but by bandwidth.

Here's a radical idea based on my Most Important Road Trip Rule from a couple chapters back. Whenever you are en route in the car *anywhere* with your kids—be it for vacation, car pool, a dentist appointment, or to Grandma's house—allow no cell phones, video, audio, or other electronic distractions for you or your kids. It's okay to listen to music or the ball game together; the key word is *together*. And it's still okay to bring the dog.

Without the isolating gadgets, you'll have to resort to talking to each other. And teasing and laughing together. Is it okay for the kids to watch a movie together in the backseat while you're driving? Not for my money. How many captive moments with your kids can you afford to lose? Looking back someday, wouldn't you rather have been talking or singing or playing a word game?

For vacations, the beauty of camping or beach trips is that the connections to the outside world often fail at remote locations, so you don't have to be the bad guy who says, "Turn that off." You and your kids can concentrate on the setting and scenery, and enjoy the family bond and spirit that spending intimate time together creates, without digital interruptions. Now, imagine the possibilities of no social media, email, videos, or text messaging even for the more mundane travel required for running errands or commuting to after-school activities. Those trips are short enough that your kids will learn to do without the digital crutches of perpetual connectivity. Face time between you and your kids trumps FaceTime and Facebook with others, even if it's only a short reprieve.

There's also a potentially life-saving benefit to unplugging in the car. Talking and texting on cell phones while driving causes fatal traffic accidents, second only to driving under the influence. You may think that it's okay for *you* to talk and drive because *you* are a much too careful and experienced driver to be easily distracted while driving. But even if you think of yourself as talented enough to juggle the phone, steer the wheel, put on the brakes, check the side and rearview mirrors, and monitor the traffic flow while talking or texting, is that the kind of behavior you want your kids to mimic someday when they drive? Remember, they are watching you. When you teach them that the car is an unplugged zone, you'll capture precious moments with them that otherwise would have been lost to digital distractions. And unplugging will become a habit, just like putting on a seat belt, which will make them safer someday soon when they get behind the wheel themselves.

By the time your kids get home from their unplugged travel, they will undoubtedly be going through withdrawal. Recognize that they need to reestablish their networks, and give them some unstructured time, space, and privacy to log back on.

You probably need to check your messages, too.

Sleepaway Camp Runamok

Important disclaimer: For those of you who are lifelong summer sleepaway camp families, please skip this chapter, or be forewarned and forgive me in advance for what I'm about to tell you. My goal in writing this book is to give you new ideas and new approaches to finding time with your kids, not to disrupt family traditions that work well for you. You needn't fix what's not broken. But, that said . . .

I am not a fan of sleepaway camps. Soon enough your kids will move out—to college or to life's other endeavors that take them from you and your home. Why send them away prematurely? Sleepaway camp is like short-term boarding school. It is true that camp is a great experience for kids. It teaches them independence, self-reliance, interpersonal and social skills, and how to squat over a toilet seat to avoid physically touching anything in those disgusting bathrooms. And the friendships at sleepaway camp are intense and often lifelong. But kids can get almost all of those same benefits at day camp and still come home for dinner every night, where they can share the experiences of their day with you, and vice versa. Kids can eat camp food, sing camp songs, play camp pranks—and still be home for a bedtime story and kiss goodnight.

Summers are important times in your family's life. Yes, you still have to work, and the kids still need to be happily occupied during the day. But without the burden of homework and the rigor of other school rituals, summers give your family leisurely evenings to linger over dinner on the patio, a ball game at the stadium, the short walk or drive for ice cream, or a pajama walk through the neighborhood.

Day camps might be the best of all worlds for your family: structured time during the day when you're busy with work, and evenings all together to do the things you never take the time for during the school year. And you'll be able to afford more evening activities with all the money you'll save by not paying room and board at sleepaway camp. Why give up summer evenings with your kids by sending them away from home before you have to?

Walk, Don't Run (and Don't Drive)

*I*f someone did a study (someone probably has) on the average distance we drive with each outing, we'd surprise ourselves at how often we drive our kids short distances to "save time" and "increase efficiency." Indeed, driving can and does often save time and increase efficiency, but at what cost? The minutes we "save" by driving our kids to soccer practice at the neighborhood park are actually priceless and irreplaceable moments with them that we lose in the name of convenience.

Next time you need to take your kids somewhere nearby, walk. Walking with your kids is a great way to slow down the pace of your lives and have more unscripted moments with them. As you remember from Part 1, the "mosey button" in their brains focuses kids' attention on their time with you and on what you hope to impart to them when you're together.

Clearly, walking where you have to go is not always possible—you may have to go too far and/or need to be there too quickly. But whenever time and distance allow, walk. And while you're walking, talk—about where you're going, what you're thinking, what they're thinking, what you see on the way, what's for dinner, who said what to whom in school today. Talk about small things or big things or medium-sized things. Hold hands with your kids while you're walking if they haven't gotten too cool for that yet; if they have, put your arm around their shoulder occasionally to punctuate your conversation (and then remove your arm before any of their friends in the neighborhood see!).

The beauty of walking is that even though you may have to plan where you're going, you don't have to plan the getting there—what happens along the way is spontaneous. If you're dropping your kids off somewhere close by (a playdate, piano lessons, karate) and you would normally drive away only to return later for a pick-up, bring along a backpack with your work or reading and find a quiet place to wait until your kids are finished. The hour or two that you have alone, in a coffee shop or under a shady tree, helps you slow down, stay sane, and distance yourself a little from the pressures that would otherwise find you if you drove straight home or to work.

Then, pick up your child and walk home together!

Driver's Ed

There are important "attention buttons" that I described in Part 1 of this book that lock your kids into what they are doing and to what you are telling them; when you trigger these buttons, it helps them appreciate the special moments they spend with you. The "fun button" is among the most effective—that's the one that helps them better remember your lesson about looking both ways before crossing the street when the street you're crossing happens to lead to the ice cream store.

Adolescence can be a trying time. Kids pull back from parents and may become too cool or too busy for the usual family togetherness activities. That's normal—the teen years are a period of staggering biological and emotional changes for kids. Separation is to be expected—and is absolutely necessary to get them ready for THE moment when they leave home. But there is a simple secret for you to again become their first choice of people with whom to "hang." You haven't been this cool in their eyes since, well, those walks across the street to the ice cream store.

The simple secret? Teach your kids to drive. If leaving home for college or other young adult pursuits is THE moment (and it is), driving alone for the first time is THE mini-moment. The independence that driving brings for a child is essential preparation for the even greater independence that high school graduation brings. Just as you should be a major part of preparing your child for THE moment when you leave her for the first time in her new dorm room, you should be a major part of preparing her for THE mini-moment when she pulls out of the driveway for the first time on her own.

Not since crossing the street for tutti-frutti with sprinkles on top has your child been so excited about learning from you. Back in the day, all kids learned to drive from their parents. While many still do, driving schools have taken over the primary teaching role for families that can afford the cost and/or can't bear the stress. But even if you hire out your kids' primary driver's education to a school, you should take every chance you have to drive with them. The car key is also the key to making them want to spend every minute they can with you between the ages of fifteen and sixteen. Don't believe me? Try these magical words and see what happens: "Hey, I'm running an errand. Wanna drive?" The bedroom door flies open, the earbuds come off, and the phone gets shoved in their pocket all in the time it takes you to find your wallet.

And now you've got them right where you want them. You've pushed their attention button. They are just excited enough, and hopefully just fearful enough, to listen with rapt attention to what you tell them. Sure, you need to remind them of proper braking distance, centering the car in the lane, and avoiding the blind spot by looking over their shoulder when changing lanes. But don't miss the bigger opportunity. You have a captive audience—the last time they were so willingly trapped with you in the car was when they were buckled into their car seats eating Cheerios. At the stoplights, teach them not to enter the intersection, even when the light turns green, until they see all the cars going in the other direction have stopped . . . and then find out about school and ask about their friends. When you get to wherever your errand takes you, have them join you in the store, or at the mechanic's garage, or in the post office to continue your conversation. When you get back in the car, shift back into driver's ed mode—remind them that parking lots can be as dangerous as streets and to always watch for little kids dashing out from between the cars.

For old time's sake, before you head home, have your new driver take you to the ice cream store for tutti-frutti with sprinkles. And remind him to look both ways before turning into the drive-through. Now you've pushed his "fun button," and he's listening to every word you say.

Entertainment

Family Movie Night

Take this as the cultural challenge of our times—finding movies that are appropriate and enjoyable for everyone in the family. Like taco night and minor holidays, family movie nights can be *little* big events—times with the kids that take little planning, little money, and little energy while producing *big* memories. Going out to the movies is fun but can be expensive. There are so many streaming alternatives today that the only trick left to seeing movies as a family is picking the right one. Moviemakers have keyed in on this challenge and have found a way to turn it very profitable; today's slick animated films are targeted to both adult and kid sensibilities. Some of the jokes are way above a younger child's head, and the story lines may be as well, but there are also enough cute characters, goofy gags, and slapstick to tickle a wide range of childhood maturity levels.

Choosing the right movie becomes another chance to spend precious moments with your kids. Instead of screening all the movies yourself, involve your kids in the process of picking age-appropriate films that appeal to the genre preferences for all of the kids. For nights when those slick animated films don't make the cut, action fans may have to watch "RomComs," and vice versa—but never compromise on the idea that everyone watches together. This is also a chance to force a little culture on your kids—occasionally, make them watch a "classic," because no child should ever graduate from high school without having seen *Casablanca*, *West Side Story*, *The Sound of Music*, *Butch Cassidy and the Sundance Kid*, and *Singin' in the Rain*.

If you're watching at home, enforce the movie theater rule—no cell phones allowed. Make sure you pop the popcorn and fetch the snacks before the movie starts to mimic the theatergoing fun. And then, most importantly, after it's over, whether you've been in the theater or at home, conduct a formal review process where each child turns movie critic. Everyone has to "score" the movie on a one to ten scale, or grade it "A" through "F," and give reasons for their rating. The idea is not to debate which score is right or wrong, but rather to teach your kids to give, and let you receive, honest feedback on their tastes and preferences. Don't give your own rankings, because if your score is closer to one of your kids' ratings than to another, it will look like you're taking sides or that there is a "right" answer. Scoring a movie teaches your kids to formulate and express their opinions without embarrassment or fear of "being wrong." Rotate the order of asking your kids for their ranking—but start with the youngest more often, lest he always pick the same score as his older sibs. Scoring is your chance to see what tickles their funny bones, or scares the daylights out of them, or makes them think. It's also a guide for you in choosing future family movie night entertainment. But best of all, it's another excuse to share time with your kids even after the credits roll.

Your kids will also be watching movies without you—perhaps with their siblings or friends, or even alone during downtime. The same principles apply—popcorn, no cell phones, and scoring—discuss the movie with your child afterward, how does she score it, and what did she like or dislike about it. Would she watch it again? (For the youngest kids, the answer to that is always "yes please, Mommy!" Older kids are a little more discriminating.)

The real motive for seeing movies as a family, of course, is that your kids are the only ones who can figure out how to work the remote.

Singing and Dancing with the Stars

Television talent competitions have become popular family entertainment because each family member can pick their own favorite performers and root for them—whom your kids root for gives you insight into their tastes and development, indirectly expressing their "rating" (see previous chapter, "Family Movie Night," and next chapter, "TV (and Other Screen) Guide"). But why stop with just *watching* the stars sing and dance?

Make your kids laugh listening to your karaoke version of songs from their favorite movies and watching you bust a move to oldies music of your generation. Teach them the great music from your generation and the great music you love from your parents' generation—kids should know the Beatles, the Temptations, the Rolling Stones, the Supremes, and Simon and Garfunkel—and the most fun way for them to appreciate great artists of the past is to watch you rock and roll. Ask your kids to rate your performance as they rate the movies and TV shows you watch with them—but don't be insulted by their rating, just *pretend* you are; half the fun is your faux-pouting when they score you a two out of ten. "Oh yeah?" you complain. "Let's see you do better!" That's when your kids really show off and you reluctantly score them an eight out of ten, allowing them to gloat and trash-talk you.

And that's how they learn to love the Beatles. And Lady Gaga, Beyoncé, Bruno Mars, and Coldplay.

TV (and Other Screen) Guide

Because there are so many better activities to share with kids, you probably assumed TV wouldn't make it into this book, and you certainly wouldn't expect an endorsement for YouTube, TikTok, Instagram, Reddit, and untold other social media platforms. Well, let's get real. These have become a big part of our kids' (and our) culture, bombarding our kids' (and our) phones, tablets, and laptops. Even if you try to restrict all screen time in your home or on your kids' phones, they will find it at their friends' homes or, even worse, feel like outcasts when their friends talk about the hot shows and "dope" clips online. Much as with family movie nights, TV and small screens can be our friends, and another avenue to create quality time spent together.

First, pick your favorite family TV shows. In trying to compete with streaming options, cable and network TV have become even more varied and interesting, and with even the most basic programming bundles the choices are endless. Of course, make sure your choices are age-appropriate for your kids and, ideally, suitable for everyone to watch together. When your kids are young, the shows may be animated or on the kids' channels. As your kids get older, more sophisticated fare is in order. With streaming services, you never have to all be available when the show runs, so synchronize an hour of downtime for all of you to share. Unlike family movie night, you don't need a big chunk of time to catch up with this week's thirty-minute or one-hour episode. Use family TV time as an occasional before-bedtime treat, or a perfect snowy weekend day warm-up activity after shoveling the walks. And then, like you do with family movie nights and most other activities in this book, talk about the show together. Knowing what's on TV, it's very likely the discussion will almost always be better than the show.

As with movies in the earlier chapter, your kids will also be watching TV without you—perhaps with their siblings or friends, or even alone during downtime. And, again, the same principles apply, particularly the discussions with your child afterward: ask him what he thought about the show, how he scored it, and why. These aren't lengthy discussions—a simple ranking of the show and quick explanation of the ranking tell you what you need to know and give your kids a chance to process what they watch.

Turning small screen (phones, tablets, laptops, desktop computers) offerings like YouTube, Instagram, TikTok, Reddit, Snapchat, and other social media temptations into family time is trickier but, in some ways, much more important. Sadly, your kids have access to far less appropriate viewing matter on these venues than on TV. But, on the flip side, if you can find a way to share these online posts with your kids, both the ones they find and the ones you find, the opportunities for understanding a little more of their world and their interests are worth the trouble. It is beyond the scope of this book to find the best ways to protect your kids from objectionable social media and other posts, and there are numerous parental control options. Rather, as with all the other strategies for *No Regrets Parenting*, my focus is encouraging you to turn the good, funny, wholesome, and entertaining small screen posts into meaningful family time. More about that in the upcoming chapter "Social Media." But for now, suffice it to say that online videos should be treated like Family Movie Night and TV time—pick the entertainment with your kids, watch together, and then have your kids give the clips a ranking. These are usually short in length, and it might work better to rank the entire evening's selections as a whole—you can tell by their laughter (or groans) how they feel about each individual post.

Finally, setting limits on your kids' screen time—all types, including social media interactions with friends, phone use, and even educational apps (see upcoming chapter, "Video Games—When in Rome")—is one of the great challenges for parents. Every family situation is different, and there is no "one-size-fits-all" solution. I refer you to the American Academy of Pediatrics statements and "toolbar" on this issue.* These recommendations are a true testimony to the times—prior AAP recommendations were much more restrictive regarding screen time for kids of all ages, and then we pediatricians got real. You might consider a "screen contract" or at least a "phone contract" with your kids to codify the rules. Contracts, even among loving family members, help to establish the importance of rules.

But it's not enough to limit your kids—as with everything else about *No Regrets Parenting*, you have to be the role model for them and abide by the rules you've set. At least when they're around, you shouldn't be glued to your screens (and it's probably not a bad idea to detach yourself a bit even when the kids aren't watching . . . just sayin').

* https://services.aap.org/en/news-room/news-releases/aap/2016/aap-announces-new-recommendations-for-media-use/

* https://www.aap.org/en-us/advocacy-and-policy/aap-health-initiatives/Pages/Media-and-Children.aspx

Family University

TV game and quiz shows have permeated our society so thoroughly that it seems like we ought to get something redeeming back in exchange for all the flashing lights, clanging bells, and celebrity blather we and our kids are exposed to. Enter Family University. Rather than everyone zoning out while watching TV's spinning wheels, weakest links, and deals (or no deals), design and play your own "game show" that's tailored to perfectly fit your kids' knowledge and interest levels. Play Family University after dinner, on weekends, before bedtime, and especially during summers when your kids' brain activity is at its nadir.

Your kids are the contestants. It's easy to find quiz questions for kids—use their schoolbooks, check out subject review books from the library, or go online to find sample questions from all the standardized tests your kids have to take. But don't limit yourself to school subjects—make it more fun by mixing in questions about movie and music stars, cartoon characters, your kids' favorite storybooks, TV shows, and anything else that captures their fancy. You can get lots of ideas, and already-written questions at age-appropriate levels, on the games shelf at the toy store. Look for trivia and brain teaser games, flash card sets, and home versions of those TV quiz shows we're avoiding. There are also online (of course!) quiz competitions for kids against other kids *not* in your family. The point is not to sterilize your kids' fun or immunize them against popular media and culture (see the previous two chapters)—the point is to take them away from the TV and put them right in front of you, laughing and learning.

And when your family quiz show gets old, create Family University "laboratories" to keep your kids motivated to learn while having fun. Some examples: use Google Maps to find your home, neighborhood, city, and country; use Legos or building blocks to create cityscapes; explore space with the NASA website; make a homemade weather station (instructions online) and follow online weather maps to track hurricane paths; build a terrarium. Perform kitchen chemistry: make a geyser by dropping Mentos in a bottle of Coke or a volcano with baking soda and vinegar; create an oil and water lava lamp; write secret messages with lemon-juice invisible ink; make "slime" with three simple ingredients.

Learning in Family University shouldn't feel like learning. Make it so fun that your kids will want to re-enroll.

High School Musical
(and High School Football)

The best family entertainment buys of today are brought to you by your neighborhood high school. For a few bucks, and often for free, you can take your kids to see classic Broadway shows; varsity sports; holiday concerts; competitions in geography, math, speech, and engineering; and debates and cooking contests. High school events provide a wholesome opportunity for parents of pre-high school kids to take advantage of the natural idolization young kids have for older kids. For a seven-year-old baseball fan, the local high school baseball team is perfect entertainment—and most schools even sell hot dogs. Does your daughter love *High School Musical* and its many sequels, spin-offs, and copycats? Take her to the next high school musical! Is your middle schooler a math and science whiz? Take her to the next bridge-building or egg drop contest at the high school. Check your local high school's website for upcoming events.

The best part for parents comes afterward, when you and your kids can discuss your favorite scene in the school play, the razzle-dazzle quarterback option play, the merits of each side of the debate, or the coolest bridge design. It's during these post-event moments that your kids and you get an early insight into what their future high school interests might be.

Alas, what if your kids are already *in* high school and they attend their school events with friends rather than with you? Take them to local *college* events! Even the coolest high school basketball player or cheerleader will want to see what's next—how does college basketball or cheerleading compare with high school? Take your high schooler to the college game (or musical) this weekend, and buy him a soft pretzel to chew on while you discuss . . . your favorite scene in the play, the razzle-dazzle quarterback option play, the merits of each side of the debate, or the coolest bridge design. And yes, it's during these post-event moments that your high schoolers and you get an early insight into what their future *college* and *career* interests might be.

The Library (or Bookstore)

*I*n an era of unlimited online access to information and literature, teach your kids to love libraries—offline! These are wonderful places with unlimited opportunities for sharing, browsing, sitting on laps, reading stories, and learning the value of free entertainment. A library card should be the first thing you put in your child's first wallet. Find your favorite spot in the library, and go there often. When your kids are younger, their favorite spot is likely in the kids' section. As they get older, it may be in the cushy chairs next to the new-fiction shelves. Sometimes you may want to take your work and their homework to the library if everyone needs a change of venue for the daily routines.

Libraries come in branches, close to home. But the best part about libraries is that the reading selection is different than in your home. The second-best part is that the books are free—find the ones they love, check them out, read them over and over together for a couple weeks, and then swap them for a new set. Yes, many books are also available inexpensively or free online, but don't you and your kids have enough screen time? Kids should learn to love books, actual books they can hold as they manually turn the pages. I watched a child sitting with a book on her mother's lap in the waiting room of my clinic, moving her fingers apart as if she were enlarging the screen on an iPad. It made me sad.

Bookstores can serve similar purposes of together time with special spots for reading—the small independents have little reading nooks, but even the big-box stores often have cushy chairs scattered about.

Some of the stores even have your favorite gourmet coffee nearby. Of course, the bookstore books aren't free, but once you find the ones your kids love, remember the titles for their birthday and holiday gifts.

However you choose to use your time in the library or bookstore, the outcome is always good: it's time with your kids, reinforcing the joys of reading, showing them you love reading, and serving up plenty of lively discussions and idea-sharing—and more insight into how your kids think about things. All this, and no admission fee required.

Play

Personal Trainer and Coach

Teach your kids to play sports. It's fair to assume, I think, that most of you are not professional athletes. But there is a magical stage in your kids' growth and development where you are better at sports than they are. Warning: That stage doesn't last very long for most of us, so you should take advantage of it while it lasts. The beauty of teaching sports to kids is that it is an intimate, healthy, and fun interaction that requires no set time, no special location, and no expense other than the cost of a volleyball, baseball mitt, or tennis racket. Even if you haven't bounced a ball since your own childhood, you start out being better than your kids at just about any sport. Try several sports and see which of them your kids (and you) enjoy the most. Kick the ball around when you get home from work; throw a softball while waiting for the school bus with your kids in the morning; shoot hoops at the park on weekends.

Before you know it, your kids may show a talent for one of the sports you've tried with them—or they may have no talent at all but just enjoy playing the game. That's the time to transition to an organized neighborhood program that can teach kids more than you can about the sport and let them socialize with other kids who are making the same transition. Encourage your kids to play hard, and teach them what it means to be a good sport. Use sports as a teaching tool for life lessons. Winning and losing. Self-improvement. Trying your best. Being part of a team. Overcoming disappointment. Dealing with people who can be difficult.

When your kids start neighborhood or school sports, it doesn't mean your job is done. Get to your kids' games when you can, continue playing and practicing the sport with them, and warm up with them in the backyard or at the park before driving them to their games—at least until they start throwing the ball so hard you might get hurt! If you have the time, help coach the team; coaching is a wonderful example of the subliminal togetherness strategy I described in Part 1 of this book. Your child is part of a team, interacting with friends, oblivious to the fact that her parent is there with her—in her eyes, you're the coach, but your eyes still get to see your little star in action.

It's also important to know when your kids should *stop* neighborhood or school sports. The rule for stopping is simple: stop when it's no longer fun for them. As kids get older, the competitiveness and intensity of sports may get to be too much, but your kids may be hesitant to tell you if they think you want them to keep playing. *No Regrets Parenting* is about really knowing your kids. This is no exception—be with them enough to know what they're enjoying and what they're not enjoying.

Other Pastimes

I don't like the word "pastimes" because it sounds as if the goal of these activities is to pass time, which seems so wasteful when time with your kids is so fleeting and precious. The goals of *No Regrets Parenting* are to maximize and optimize time lest it pass too quickly. Having said that, participating in pastimes with your kids can be very meaningful if you don't take the word too literally. Think of pastimes as "share times" with your kids, leisurely activities for you and your kids to do together.

If your kids don't take to sports (see the previous chapter), fear not. Many relationships between parents and kids turn out just fine even without the bleacher blisters and sideline screaming that come with sports as your kids grow older and the competition heats up. Help your kids find other interests that you can be a part of, too—theater, scouting, dance, writing, art, music. These are a little harder for you to coach if you're not an actor, Eagle Scout, dancer, writer, artist, or musician. Unlike sports, you may *never* be better than your kids at these pastimes, and getting your kids started can be a little less spontaneous and requires a little more planning. But that doesn't mean you can't get them started. Encourage your kids to try out for neighborhood and high school theater productions and concerts. Start a family blog and have your kids write their own entries. Many schools offer after-school enrichment programs for nominal cost: dance, karate, drawing, science, etc. Then, when you and your kids are home together, have them show you what they've learned; let your kids be your teachers for these activities; practice with them.

A cautionary note is in order regarding pastimes, lest you become a "potpourri parent." That's the term I used in Part 1 of this book to describe the syndrome of uber-parenting that relentlessly thrusts kids into a highly programmed "*if-it's-Tuesday-it-must-be-violin-lessons-because-figure-skating-is-not-till-Wednesday*" schedule. Potpourri parents subject their kids to constant activity in the hope that their kids will discover their innermost passion—the never-ending search for an experiential epiphany. Kids of potpourri parents are far too busy for parents to meaningfully share the activities with them. That should not be the goal of pastimes.

As with everything else in *No Regrets Parenting*, sharing pastimes with your kids requires balance along with your observational skills and intuition. When you are attuned to your kids' reactions, and you're with your kids often enough to see those reactions, you'll learn what they enjoy, what they're good at, and what gives them a sense of accomplishment. Along the way, since you're sharing the pastime with your kids, you may even learn to sing or dance a little yourself (see earlier chapter, "Singing and Dancing with the Stars").

Hobby Sharing

*I*f you have a hobby, share it with your kids. If you don't have a hobby, kids are a great excuse to develop one. Hobbies can be the ultimate playdate and another activity for you to "double dip," doing things with your kids that you all enjoy equally. When they are young, your kids will enjoy whatever hobby you enjoy. If you think it's cool, they'll think it's cool, and they'll love being part of your playtime. By the time they get a little older, even if your stamp or coin collection becomes passé for them, you've still had meaningful time together and they have a deeper appreciation for what makes you tick. Especially if your hobby is fixing antique clocks. Sorry. ☺

While philately and numismatics may or may not capture your older kids' fancy, many adult hobbies are very cool even for the coolest kids. Drones, radio-controlled cars (or boats and planes), fantasy sports (but not the gambling kind), jewelry design, fishing, computer geek stuff, cake design, model cars and planes, moviemaking, electric trains, all-terrain vehicles, pottery, magic, sailing, origami, scrapbooking, beadwork, photography . . . the list of cool hobbies goes on and on. Kids of all ages can share your passions for cooking and gardening. Make your kids part of your meal preparation, teach them to follow recipes and add ingredients, and then let them serve the product at dinner with pride. Spring vegetable gardening (and fall harvesting) is a great hobby to share and a great opportunity to teach a little about nature and biology. Kid favorites to pick are tomatoes, cherry tomatoes, cucumbers, snap peas, pumpkins, and squash; favorites to dig up are potatoes, carrots, and radishes.

If you're picking a new hobby to grow into with your kids, there are several factors to consider in your choice. First, your new hobby should be fun and stimulating for you so you'll stick with it; if you give up on your hobby, or flit from one fad to another, your kids will lose interest and you'll send them the wrong message about following through on projects and commitments. Second, make sure the new hobby is safe for them to continue on their own when they're a little older; your schedules won't always synchronize, and if you are lucky and pick a hobby that your kids really love, they will want to do it on their own when you're busy or share it with their friends. For that reason, welding, electrical repair, taxidermy, and meat smoking might not be the best choices. Third, pick a conveniently located and easily accessible hobby. One of the best benefits of sharing a new hobby with your kids is that it helps you make the most of your time with them whenever that time pops up. Calendars and advance scheduling are very important for sharing planned moments with your kids, but occasionally surprises occur—soccer practice is rained out, your business meeting is postponed, or their school declares a snow day. If your hobby requires a long drive to the lake, the rock-climbing hill, or the skeet-shooting range, you probably won't make the effort with short notice or a brief window of time. But if everything you need is in the garage, the kitchen, the family room, or just a short drive away, you and your kids can have fun spontaneously, as soon as the opportunity occurs. Finally, pick a hobby that's cool enough that your kids may even choose to do it with you over the option of watching TV or playing video games alone in their room. Which brings up the obvious question: What about picking video games as your hobby to share with kids? For more on that, see the next chapter.

Now that you've involved your kids in your hobby or picked a new hobby to master together, you have to promise not to sneak off too often to play alone while they're in school!

Video Games—When in Rome

I am not a fan of video games for kids. I read all the arguments in favor of them, trying to be responsive and fair to my kids' pleading when they were young. But I'm unconvinced that the hand-eye coordination and tech savvy supposedly gained by these games can't be better gained with other activities (although I have to admit, I think I remember my mother telling me the same thing about my childhood addiction to pinball machines). That said, our family boycott of Xbox, PlayStation, and Wii products didn't work out so well. Every other kid in the neighborhood, and in every other neighborhood, had those diabolical digital devices. Those devices aren't even necessary any longer because video games are now easily downloaded and played on TV, computer, digital devices, and phone screens. They can be handheld and easily concealed in classrooms and under the dinner table. Video games are inescapable. But our video game–less home was not inescapable—our kids simply escaped to their friends' houses, where they spent playdate hours making up for lost time. So . . . when in Rome, you may have to do as the Romans do, lest all the Romans defect to Greece, if you know what I mean.

When you do decide to cave in (note I didn't say, "*If* you do decide . . ."—for most of you, it's probably a foregone conclusion) and bring the magic of video games into your home, at least do your best to screen the games and, gasp, maybe even learn them so you can experience this part of your kids' free time with them, too. Does playing video games with your kids qualify as quality time?

Setting personal bias aside, I have to say, yes, when seen through a *No Regrets Parenting* lens. First, your kids will kick your butt; this is one activity where you'll never have to *let* them win, and it's a good thing for kids to occasionally see their parents as human and vincible. Second, there will be guaranteed hilarity at your lack of dexterity; your lack of prosperity (these devices and downloads are not cheap) won't be as funny. Finally, some games have somewhat-redeeming virtual realities because they closely mimic real-world activities such as table tennis, bowling, baseball, skiing, and dancing (which are much better, in my mind, than games where you blow each other up). Of course, those video games that mimic real-world activities beg the question: Why not just do the real versions of table tennis, bowling, baseball, skiing, and dancing? But there's my bias again.

Bottom line: when video games become important to your kids (again, note I didn't say "*If* video games become important to your kids") and you can afford to indulge them, suck it up and try to see the games as just another route for getting closer to your kids and their world.

Educational game apps are a category unto themselves and, while likely to be *your* first choices for your kids' screen time, they will likely have to be an acquired taste for your kids, who would prefer Minecraft and Fortnite. Educational apps are available in every possible subject: reading, writing, spelling, science, math, geography, music, art, history, the stock market, etc. ad infinitum! Screen educational apps—and all online activities for kids—carefully for age-appropriateness, and avoid those with advertisements and/or "in-game" purchases. Most importantly, screen them carefully to make sure your kids will have fun with them, lest online learning becomes a chore rather than enjoyment.

And, as with all screen time (see earlier chapter, "TV (and Other Screen) Guide"), set limits, lest their virtual realities take over their reality.

Online Creativity

Thankfully, video games are not the only way for you and your kids to share online experiences. Much as you'll read in the "Social Media" chapter later, online opportunities have exploded for kids and their parents to be creative, have fun together, and grow. From the longstanding kids' websites like Sesame Street, Crayola, and National Geographic Kids, to the hundreds of new sites that have popped up for kids' art, writing, puzzles, and games, safe online choices for nurturing kids' ingenuity and curiosity abound. Show your pride in your kids' online work as you would the pictures they draw and stories they write with real crayons and pencils—print them, post them on your fridge, frame the best ones, and send them to grandparents.

You and your kids can also share the online apps and websites you use to express *your* creativity (or do your job) like PowerPoint, Photoshop, Visme, Google Docs and Google Slides, Excel, and Prezi. Teach your kids how to make presentations, create photo displays and spreadsheets, write stories and storybooks, and create animation. And then, after they've spent a few minutes learning, let them show you how to do all those things even better. Kids are so facile with technology; you just need to give them access—safe access—and they'll love making you feel like a Luddite as their fingers dance across the keyboard.

Interactive creativity with your kids online is another wonderful way to share quality time even if you're not in the same room at the same time. All of your grown-up creativity apps and websites, and many of your kids' resources, allow for group participation and contributions. Design progressive art, write progressive stories, or compose progressive music online, where you and your child take turns adding to the pieces. Do it on your work breaks and add to the fun by video "conferencing" with your child as you add your parts, or do it sitting side-by-side with your child at home after dinner.

Toy Story and Game Theory

*I*f you're able to avoid the video game lure, and even if you succumb to it, your choices of non-digital games and toys for your kids are plentiful—kids are a big, big market. Choose carefully. There are several goals to strive for in picking playthings for your kids. First, they should be affordable; second, they should lend themselves to play both with and without you. That is, you want to pick toys and games you can play with your kids and that kids can play on their own when you're busy. Finally, the items you pick for your kids should encourage communication and interaction—solitary play is okay once in a while and helps build independence, but group play is more than play; it's socialization. And when you're part of the group, it's quality time with your kids.

Board games, on real boards, are fabulous for kids and for your relationship with your kids, regardless of their age. From Candy Land and Monopoly, to checkers and chess, to Scrabble and Catan, playing board games with your kids gives you access and insight into their thought processes and imaginations. Watch them scheme and strategize, see their competitive streaks gently peek out, and teach them the lessons of graceful losing and humble winning. Card games have many of the same advantages as board games and are even less expensive. You don't need pricey (and often presumptuous) "educational toys" to teach your kids the valuable lessons learned by interacting with others, nor should you feel that play always needs to be enlightening. Fun can just be fun, and playing with you is always fun for your kids.

Simple dolls and toy trucks lead to creative play and storytelling with your kids. Perhaps the best toys of all are the "character" toys crafted from popular TV shows like *Sesame Street* or from Disney and superhero movies. These hard rubber statuettes (or, if your kids prefer, soft stuffed characters) encourage your kids to mimic the characters' voices and dialogue in made-up scenarios and homegrown scripts. Every evening's storyline can be different. Your kids can play among themselves or with friends, but whenever you can join the performance, jump right in. You'll usually be assigned to play the "bad guy" to your kids' superheroes, but don't you often feel like that's your role in the family anyway? ☺

Outdoors

Just a Walk in the Park (or Zoo)

*Y*our tax dollars are nowhere better spent than on the creation and maintenance of public parks and zoos. Whether you have your own big backyard or live on the fifteenth floor of a high-rise, parks provide special moments with your kids that other settings can't match for the price (free!). Well, yes, there are the taxes, but you have to pay those whether you take advantage of the parks or not, so you might as well take advantage.

Picnics, soccer matches or softball games for playing or watching, baseball fields, basketball and tennis courts, climbing towers with slides, monkey bars, and swing sets. And each piece of equipment, playing field, stretch of grass, or walking trail provides new opportunities for chatter, laughter, and memory-making with your kids. Which park was it where you taught your daughter to swing a tennis racket, and how many times were you able to ping the ball back and forth during that first lesson? On which hoop did you teach your son to make a lay-up? Which was the best sledding hill? The perfect picnic spot? Isn't that the tree our kite got stuck in? Remember feeding the ducks on the pond? Or how we collected the prettiest leaves during fall?

Winter transforms parks into something entirely wondrous! Have snowball fights (or snowball target practice against tree trunks), make snow angels, build snowpersons and snow forts. Play snow-Frisbee or snow-football. Snowshoe, sled, and cross-country ski across the park. Make snow art with diluted food coloring in squirt bottles and blow

196 NO REGRETS PARENTING

snow bubbles. (Bubbles from regular bubble solution freeze in the cold, land, and can be picked up!)

If you are close enough, walk or bike to the park to extend the serenity of the day. Parks are also a great place for applying the "subliminal togetherness" strategy with your kids (see Part 1). Depending on their age, you can turn them loose to play on their own, socialize with other kids, explore their environment, play sports—all with you hovering just far enough away that they can develop their independence without noticing your watchful presence. Bring a book and find a shady tree where you have a great view of their growth and maturation.

Is there any place as fun for young kids as the zoo? The time you spend strolling past the animals, pointing fingers, and laughing at the silly-looking Malayan tapir or the scary Abyssinian hornbill—or the gigantic elephant poop!—is pure and wholesome entertainment of the non-video game, non-TV type. Have everyone pick their favorite reptiles or choose names for the monkeys (your kids may *not* use their siblings' names in this game!). All of the same togetherness benefits of the zoo can be found at the aquarium if your town has one. When your kids are a little older, the botanical gardens may catch their fancy, although funny ferns are not nearly as captivating as furry friends for most kids.

Hooked at the Hip

*I*n Part 1 of this book, I describe "double dipping" as a strategy for spending more quality time with your kids while still taking care of yourself and staying sane. The "double dipping" approach is to find activities that you and your kids would enjoy doing *without* each other and then do them together. There are lots of examples throughout the book. But outdoor activity and exercise offer the most options for "double dipping." Why? Because so many of the most popular and healthy forms of exercise can be tailored to your fitness goals *and* to your kids' ability level.

BIKING. You can't beat bikes for inexpensive and healthy double dipping. Devices now exist to take kids of almost any age along for the ride—from trailers, to trailer cycles, to "pre-bikes," to tandem bikes. And, of course, when the kids are big enough, they get their own set of wheels to ride alongside you. Explore different trails to keep it interesting for you and an adventure for your kids. Read a map with your older kids and plan the route together; when they're still hooked up to your bike in a trailer, talk to them as you're riding and tell them where you're riding. Teach them trail etiquette and turn signals. Play I Spy, or the "hold your breath, here comes a bump" game, or count how many animals they can spot along the way. Exercise, fresh air, and fresh scenery!

SWIMMING. When your kids are little, they need full-time supervision in the pool, so bring an adult buddy who also has kids, and tag team—you swim laps while your buddy makes sure all the water wings are in place, and then he swims while you're on pool-noodle duty. As your kids get older, they can play with friends while you exercise in the pool. If adult lap hours are different than open swim hours, start a personal water aerobics program for yourself to keep moving while your kids swim; then when lap time begins, sit them down with a snack on the pool chairs.

JOGGING/WALKING. Like bike trailers, jogging strollers let you bring even the littlest ones along for the run. Or let your "middle-age" kids bike alongside as you jog. If you have a dog, this becomes "triple dipping"!

KARATE LESSONS. If you and your kids are beginners, find a martial arts sensei (teacher) who will let you take lessons together. But when it gets to the learning level where you are paired off for fighting matches, it's probably a good idea to ask for an unrelated opponent.

SNOWSHOEING. Skiing and snowboarding are great if you live near the mountains and can afford the lift tickets. But the youngest kids aren't allowed on the slopes, and toddlers and "middle-age" kids are usually relegated to the bunny slopes, far from where you'd like to be skiing. Much less expensive than skiing, though, and without the requirement of a mountain, snowshoeing is invigorating winter exercise for almost all ages, and all you need is a nearby park (see previous chapter). As the slogan goes, anyone who can walk can snowshoe. And for your pre-walkers and toddlers who tire quickly, put them in a sled hooked up to a waist leash and pull them behind you.

HIKING. This one is actually easiest when your kids are little and can fit in a Snugli or backpack child carrier. The whining doesn't usually start until your kids *can* walk but would much prefer walking in the mall. A few hiking hacks might help—first, don't call a hike a hike; call it a nature adventure or an outdoor treasure hunt. A second sometimes-helpful solution to the "I don't wanna go" problem returns to a tried-and-true parenting strategy—bribery. Lollipops, licorice sticks, gorp with M&M's, and other trail treats (okay, okay—sliced apples, raisins, and Fruit Roll-Ups *may* work as carrots to move your kids along the trail. Carrots themselves, however, not so much). Gear can help—canteens, compasses, pedometers, and binoculars are kid favorites. Be creative—collect pine cones or pretty rocks along the trail, find branches for walking sticks, skip rocks on ponds and lakes, birdwatch. And when the kids are a little older, try geocaching—the ultimate in treasure hunts.

ROWING. For kids younger than teens, it's best to keep canoe, kayak, and rowboat outings limited to gentle lakes and streams rather than raging rivers. But the aerobic and upper-body workout for you is still fantastic. Kids of all ages love getting out on the water enough to happily put on their life jackets.

FISHING. Casting flies into a pristine lake or mountain river with your kids offers a whole new angle to the term "double dipping." The moments and memories you snag will be much more meaningful for all of you than anything that ends up on your line. But if something does end up on your kid's line, take pictures!

ROLLERBLADING AND ROCK CLIMBING. Some adult outdoor fitness activities can be a little tricky with kids of certain ages. These two are clearly not options where you can include infants the way you can with biking and jogging, and it's hard to safely skate or climb alongside young kids who are just learning. Some "double dipping" may prove to be "double slipping (and falling)" for many families, but may work well for yours.

You already know how great you feel after exercising outdoors; as further proof, numerous studies have found significant mental and physical health advantages of outdoor workouts compared with those in the gym. And those studies don't even mention the "parental mental" health benefits of knowing that you have captured precious, sweaty moments with your kids.

Geese and Sunsets—"Wowwww, Dad!"

*H*ow old were you when you first noticed a beautiful sunset, the gentle and graceful flight of geese, or the shadows on the walls of the Grand Canyon at dusk? When did you first marvel at the palette of fall trees, the snowcapped peaks, or the spray from the ocean hitting the shore? I can tell you one thing—it wasn't during your childhood.

Kids have a dense filter covering their eyes and a barricade in their brains that somehow let them wander through life without being awed, or even aware, of the natural beauty around them. Mountain lakes, galaxy-filled nighttime skies, wildflowers in bloom? Nope. Kids don't see the forest *or* the trees! Well, that's not entirely true. Kids do notice ants. And spiders.

The disconnect between adults hoping to imbue their kids with an appreciation for the wonders around them, and kids who seemingly couldn't care less, can be disconcerting for parents. Our kids developed the annoying (but admittedly very cute) custom of responding to our "Hey, isn't that waterfall gorgeous?" with "Wowwww, Dad," droned in an unimpressed and pseudo-bored cacophony. At least their response confirmed they were occasionally awake on our hikes in the national parks.

So, what's a parent to do when your best efforts to make outdoor moments special with your kids are rewarded with a collective yawn? Expect it, accept it, and be comforted by two important truths: first, what makes your moments with your kids special is not the scenery—it's the company; and second, kids *do* absorb your enthusiasm and energy, even if they miss the bluebirds and the lily pads. They'll balk at hiking, but they'll remember that their moments in the woods were fun because they were with you, sleeping in a tent, roasting marshmallows, eating s'mores, and telling stories. They'll remember the big rocks that they thought were bears, the tree roots they thought were snakes, stopping at the drive-through for root beer, and being grossed out at the camper dump site. Yes, they'll ignore the full harvest moon, the rainbows, and the fossils and fault lines in the hillside rocks, but at least they won't be playing video games or online chatting in their room. They'll be with you, in the fresh air, doing things you can feel good about.

And then, sometime in late adolescence or early adulthood, a magical awakening occurs. The fog in their brains clears, and they start to notice the beauty of the world around them without your having to narrate or nag.

That's when you show them the pictures to prove they were on this trail before, with you.

Communication

Shareholder Meetings

*I*f things are running smoothly in a household, families should be meeting all the time. Often those encounters don't involve everyone at once and are on the fly—in the car en route to school or errands; doing the microwave mambo before work; during bath time and bedtime rituals. Those fleeting meetings typically deal with immediate and practical issues like who's driving whom where and when, whose turn in the bathtub, what time judo class is over today, and what we should do for dinner tonight.

The most important and recurrent meetings are during the one mealtime when everyone sits down together; those gatherings firmly anchor the family, sharing the happenings of the day, setting the plans for tomorrow, and dealing with the little issues that crop up all the time (see earlier chapter, "The Daily Dinner Meeting").

But periodically, there are circumstances when formal "shareholder meetings" are necessary. In the corporate world, shareholders (those who hold a stake in the company) are called together to discuss the big things: earnings and dividends, mergers and acquisitions, advances in research and development, the election of new board members, etc. The business of being in a family is also serious and important enough to, on an as-needed basis, hold meetings that include everyone in the family, regardless of age. All the shareholders. This is the time for everyone to contribute, in their own way, on matters that affect the whole family or the family dynamic. Issues may include vacation planning, choice of schools, summer camp, family budgets, college and career decisions, buying a car, redecorating the house, or getting a pet. Of course, shareholder meetings are mandatory for the REALLY BIG ISSUES, like moving to a new city or changes in the family structure (marriage, divorce, remarriage, a new baby on the way, the death of a grandparent).

The issues at shareholder meetings must be carefully framed in terms appropriate for your kids' ages. But even with the very youngest kids, major issues deserve a major meeting. The only way that shareholder meetings can serve their purpose is if everyone is given a chance to participate, because everyone holds a stake in the family. No opinion is unworthy; no suggestion is without merit; no concern is baseless. But to continue the corporate metaphor, parents are the CEOs, they run the shareholder meetings, and they make sure everyone has their fair say. Most importantly, the kids need to know from the outset of the meeting that the ultimate decisions regarding the big issues will be made by their parents. This is a forewarning to the kids that parents may decide something the kids disagree with, but it's also a relief for kids to know that the weight of big decisions is not on their shoulders. Kids can express their opinions freely, knowing they will be heard but will not be responsible for the outcome of the big issues.

Tell the kids they are, indeed, the family shareholders and their voices matter. Tell them you will carefully consider everything they suggest, and that your mind is not made up yet. Explain to them that you can be better parents when you know how your kids honestly feel about important family matters.

And, best of all, everything you tell them is true, which makes your family the most honest "corporation" in the world.

Photographic Memory

One of the harshest realizations for a parent is that young kids often forget those events that are the most memorable for parents. Of course, we hope our kids remember the "big picture"—that they are happy and loved and that being our kids has been a good thing for them. But there's a way to help your kids with the "little pictures" as well: by actually *showing* them the little pictures as they grow up. Maintaining a real-time photo album—hard copy or digital, on the shelf, your computer, or on your phone—allows you to sit down with your kids at quiet times and show them how cute they were when they were littler, and how much they enjoyed that special trip to Grandma's or to Disneyland. Photo albums make great bedtime stories and help long car rides and plane trips go by faster. Videos are another easy way to relive the fun moments of their younger days with your kids. Photos and videos give you an opportunity to tell them stories that they can uniquely relate to (because they are the lead characters!) and reinforce some of the happy memories they may have lost in the whirlwind that is childhood.

When they're older, it won't matter much if their recollections of childhood events are from the actual events or from your photographic retelling of those events. What will matter is that they know how they got to be who and where they are today, how much fun they had, and how much love and care went into the process. The bonus benefit is that the time you and your kids spend together revisiting the past through photos and videos will generate *new* moments of laughter and intimacy with them. And those new moments themselves will become cherished memories.

Speaking Their Language

The world is shrinking. Every day brings us closer to the international community, yet Americans remain largely monolingual. Your kids may study a second language in school, but experience suggests that most school language programs fail to produce fluent speakers. This presents another marvelous opportunity for "double dipping," participating in a worthwhile activity with your kids that is equally beneficial and enjoyable for all of you.

For the price of an inexpensive computer or phone app, you and your kids can learn a second language together. Hours in the kitchen, in the car, in doctor and dentist waiting rooms, and on airplanes can become a cultural and often comedic experience as all of you stumble over new words, experiment with new sentence structures, and cruelly mimic the faceless teacher's stiff voice.

The endpoints of this exercise are up to you. It may be just a summer's dalliance that everyone agrees has run its course by fall. Or it may lead to streaming foreign-language movies, or English-language movies that are dubbed (or subtitled) in your new tongue. It may develop into a playgroup with kids for whom your *new* language is their *first* language. You may start to read books with your kids in your second language, eat in a restaurant where they speak the language you're learning, or maybe you'll even travel together to a country where the language is spoken. Most meaningful, however, is the appreciation your kids will have for the world's diversity—kids who learn other languages and the cultures they represent become more tolerant of different perspectives and others' worldviews.

Like most undertakings with kids, the means can justify the end, whatever the end turns out to be. Learning, laughing, and sharing this new adventure together are all good, regardless of whether any of you ever *parlez, habla,* or *sprechen.*

Let "Ur" Fingers Do the Talking

There is something magical about the immediacy and efficiency of texting that makes the same kids, who will never listen to their cell phone voicemail, answer texts on the very same cell phone. Kids tolerate texting from parents—maybe because it's not very disruptive, maybe because their friends don't have to know it's you on the other end, or maybe because it speaks your kids' language better than the other ways you try to communicate with them.

And what a blessing it is that kids tolerate your texting. The worry that past generations of parents had about their kids' whereabouts and goings-on is cured, at least partially, by texting kids and simply asking, "Sup?" When they answer, and whatever their answer is, you usually know enough for now. But in addition to the tolerable leash that text messaging puts on your kids, it connects you to them at times in the day that you otherwise wouldn't be connected. After a big test, before an important game, during a teen party—you can touch base with your kids and, in addition to the actual text message that pops up on their screen, you send them an important *encrypted* message: their activities are important to you, and you are with them in spirit. Digital spirit.

Text them to be careful, to tell them what time you expect them home, and where you'll pick them up. Let them know where you are and what you're doing between now and dinner; update them on your important meeting or speech. Complain ("My boss stinks"), brag ("They loved my presentation!"), coordinate ("Dinner after lacrosse practice?").

Set the tone for family texting as open, funny, and loving—and your kids will do the same. Set up a group text that goes to everyone in your nuclear family so siblings can stay more closely connected, too. Send GIFs and emojis. Use the shorthand so your kids can tease you about your lame attempts to be cool. Texting hooks you up with your kids in real time, if only for abbreviated bursts of chat.

There is a very important additional motive to becoming regular text buddies with your kids: the habit carries over to their lives after they leave home for college or their other young adult pursuits, when texting may become your *main* form of contact with your kids.

Social Media

The greatest change in parenting (and, one could argue, the greatest change in the world) since the first edition of this book a decade ago has been the invasion and takeover of our kids' lives, and our lives, by social media. As everyone knows by now, social media can be a force for great good and for great evil. It's our job as parents to make sure our kids' social media is, if not redeeming, at least safe. Parental controls for your kids' devices are readily available, but it is beyond the scope of this book to provide comprehensive guidance for you on navigating, monitoring, and protecting your kids on these platforms. My goal here, as with all the other parts of this book, is to suggest ways to use your and your kids' social media adventures to advance the joy, and reduce the regrets, of your parenting experience. In other words, to see social media through a *No Regrets Parenting* lens.

Let me start by saying I believe social media can be a meaningful and memorable resource for *No Regrets Parenting*, but only if you share in your kids' online experiences and explorations. That doesn't mean you join in their chats with friends or even that you are their "friends" on their platforms—it means that you treat their social media interactions as you would the movies or TV shows they watch, and the video games they play, with friends. If you've read those earlier chapters, you'll recall that the discussions you have with your kids about their screen time are almost as fulfilling and insightful as watching or playing with them (although anything *with* them is better if you can).

Kids are more technically skilled than their parents; that's a fact. They embrace the latest apps, hacks, and chats before we even know they exist, and it's impossible to stop them, short of confiscating all of their devices and contacts with the outside world, so don't even try. Instead of impounding their devices, empower your kids with your wisdom and guidance. You may think you're savvy because you follow your own friends on Instagram, Twitter, or Snapchat, and you may even check in with TikTok, but have you heard of Discord, Roblox, GroupMe, Kik Messenger, Tumblr, Yubo, Amino, LiveMe, Omegle, Whisper, YouNow, MeetMe, Monkey, and Houseparty? No? Your tweens and teens have! While it's likely that by the time the Third Edition of this book comes out a few years from now, some or most of those platforms will be gone and new ones will have appeared; the point is your kids are way ahead of you and it's time to catch up. Not by downloading any or all of those apps, but by doing a gentle inventory with your kids by creating a dinner table or after dinner "chat room" of your own. Learn what your kids are doing online, ask them to show you the funniest or sweetest of their discoveries, and warn them of the dangers that may come with online "friendships."

Teach your kids to use their "spidey-sense" in identifying iffy, sketchy, or outright dangerous posts and to bring them to your attention, not only for your kids' protection but also so you can alert the hosting sites and child protection hotlines to the risk for all kids. It's not enough to block those sites from your kids' devices; the sites must be reported.

In an age-appropriate way, join your kids' social media interactions. For the youngest kids, view their screens with them, teaching with them along the way and laughing with them, too. As your kids earn more rights to privacy in their teen years, general discussions are preferable to over-the-shoulder snooping. Asking them to show you their favorite posts and pictures isn't invasive; it's sharing, because they get to choose what to show you. Repay the courtesy by sharing the posts, videos, and pictures you like on your dinosaur-era apps.

Ignoring your kids' social media adventures isn't *No Regrets Parenting*—it's naive parenting and potentially dangerous. Bullying on social media, often anonymous and always vicious, is a risk to the health and even to the lives of your kids. Talk with your kids about whom they're connecting with and explain the risks. Seemingly harmless chats can quickly deteriorate into solicitation and porn. Teach your kids never to send pictures of themselves in compromising positions or inappropriate dress. This is a difficult conversation because you're precariously teetering between becoming more involved in your kids' social media lives on the one hand, and respecting your kids' needs for privacy on the other. This conversation will often be poorly received by your kids, but it's absolutely necessary—remember, your kids are also teetering between childhood and adulthood, and they may need, if not openly welcome, your guidance here.

One way to be involved and helpful with your kids' social media use is to teach them to "check in" with themselves before logging on. Encourage them to think about why they're socializing now—is it to share, gossip, and laugh with friends, or is it "fear of missing out" or "fear of being less cool" or "fear of being less attractive?" Those "fear of" motivations for opening apps can leave kids feeling worse during, and after, their chats. So, another "check in" with themselves—or with you if they are comfortable with that—*after* their online connections can help them better understand what they're getting from social media. This is a valuable lesson in emotional awareness that will extend beyond social media to other aspects of their relationships and life experiences.

As noted in the earlier chapter "TV (and Other Screen) Guide," screen-time limits are in order and parental controls are mandatory for your younger socialites.

Long-Distance Connections

Just two generations ago, kids called home from college on Sundays because that's when the long-distance rates were cheaper. Grandparents living far from their children and grandchildren rarely saw them. Military personnel stationed far away stood in long lines for a turn to make a three-minute call to hear their loved ones' voices. Moving to another state or country meant writing letters and postcards or losing touch entirely with those who used to be close to you.

Thankfully, we've left the days when moments were lost to miles. While cell phones may have started the long-distance connectivity we enjoy today, the technology has quickly moved beyond simply being able to dial up (eek! "punch in") anyone, anywhere, and anytime at a reasonable price. Now, internet video services allow you to bring grandchildren to the computer screens of their grandparents—entirely for free! You can welcome long-ago friends back into your lives and living rooms, and conduct "face-to-face" business meetings online.

Not only does internet video bring people back into your lives and allow you stay in town for more business meetings, but it also gives you more of what *No Regrets Parenting* is all about—quality moments with your kids. When they move out for college or jobs, you'll be able to continue to be a visible part of their lives. But long before that, beginning in the crib and continuing all the way through their growing-up years, time with your kids crowded in front of the camera on your cell phone or computer-screen, or in separate little screen "boxes" on group chats, is an intimate, loving, and fun activity.

They can show off for grandparents, joke with uncles and aunts, do magic tricks for their cousins, and stay connected to friends who moved away, are sick at home, or even in the hospital. Yes, social media and texting also keep kids connected, but they do so without all the important social skills that come from face-to-face contact, albeit two-dimensional. More importantly, from a parent's perspective, when your kids communicate by text or instant message or on social media, you're usually not part of that experience with them. But when your kids are sharing the screen with you, talking to and seeing Grandma, they are sharing themselves not just with Grandma but with you, too. It's time together, you and your kids, putting on a little show and tell.

And what a godsend that is for Grandma!

Spirit and Soul

Charity Starts in the Home

There are so many people less fortunate than you and your family. Those individuals offer your kids lessons in humility and opportunities for compassion and generosity. A multitude of foundations around the country have youth boards: kids appointed to help allocate a portion of the foundation's charitable resources. The kids on these boards research potentially worthy recipients of grants and donations. This is a win-win situation—teaching tomorrow's leaders about charity as well as opening their eyes to the needy and less-advantaged in their communities. The foundations' youth boards do terrific work, but there is no reason every family shouldn't have its own youth board at home. Except for the most destitute of situations, most people give some charity every year. They may write personal checks, give at the office, bring used clothes to a collection bin, or toss coins into the cup of a person experiencing homelessness they pass on the street corner. But almost every family gives.

Giving is good. It's good for the heart and the soul, and it's good for your kids to see and experience. And, of course, it's good for the recipients of your generosity. Decide on the type and amount of charity you would like to give this year, and sit down with your kids to decide together how to distribute it. Research worthy organizations, visit local missions or shelters, decide which groups use their donations in the best way to serve their populations—and do all of that *with* your kids. When they are younger, the "research" may simply be explaining to them a little about blindness or homelessness or cancer. Talk with

222 NO REGRETS PARENTING

your kindergarten and grade school kids about donating toys they no longer play with and clothes they have grown out of to kids who aren't as lucky.

As your kids get older, they can volunteer side-by-side with you at a soup kitchen, at an abused women's shelter, or with the Special Olympics. Take a charity walk together; before you go, gather sponsors who contribute for every mile—and do that together with your kids, too. When they're old enough, your kids can volunteer on their own at the local hospital. What better way to teach them empathy and gratitude for your family's many blessings? And what better way to "double dip" (see Part 1, "Staying Sane") than doing things with your kids that are enjoyable and fulfilling for all of you. It's time spent together with your kids for the benefit of others and yourselves.

And by including your kids in acts of kindness, you amplify the good deeds that those activities produce because you are role-modeling for the next generation of compassionate givers.

Keep the Faith

Sharing your belief system with your kids is a worthwhile and meaningful expression of quality time. You may or may not observe a particular faith, and you may or may not be a spiritual person. But whatever you are, it is you. And remember that in our redefining of quality time, moments that allow your kids to better know you are precious and should be nurtured.

Sharing your beliefs with your kids will influence their beliefs just as everything you share about yourself influences them. You may want your children to accept the tenets you were taught as a child because you continue to believe in them; or, perhaps as an adult you now question those precepts but still want your kids to have the same foundation you had growing up. You may have evolved away from your own religious upbringing and found a new and meaningful belief system. Or you may not have particular religious beliefs at all, which in and of itself can be an important insight for your kids into who you are.

Often, discussing your beliefs with your kids allows you to better define those beliefs for yourself and may even renew convictions that have faded over the years. Kids are inquisitive; their questions will force you to find answers for yourself as well as for them. Whatever aspirations you have for your kids' faith, the act of sharing yourself in this way is powerful and profound. It is also at the very heart of *No Regrets Parenting*, which holds that time spent with your kids benefits them and you, and is to be cherished.

While you are sharing your belief system with your kids, take the opportunity to teach them about other faiths. Understanding the world around them requires kids to understand what others hold true and how those principles affect behaviors. If your kids ask you about a friend's or classmate's religion or philosophy of life, spend time together searching the internet for information and insight into the important foundations of people's lives. Use religious holidays, yours or others', as a starting point for discussions. Attend interfaith worship services to expose your kids to different philosophies of life.

In addition to your beliefs, share your values with your children. Religious faiths espouse strong value systems, hence bringing your child up in a particular faith will naturally expose him to the values of that faith. This book has subtly, and in some cases not so subtly, suggested certain values I feel are important for kids to learn. But the most important values for your kids to learn are not those that I suggest or even those that are attendant with your religious beliefs— unless those value reflect you and what's important to you. It's *your* values that will be passed on to your kids because they absorb them by watching you live them. Make sure your life reflects the values you want your kids to inherit. Remember our bumper sticker from earlier chapters: *Be the person you want your child to become.*

Which brings us back to *No Regrets Parenting.* When you are there for your kids, finding time for them throughout their childhood, they pattern their lives and the choices they make on the template you provide for them. Your beliefs and your values are at the core of who you are. Share them with your kids and, by doing so, you will be sharing *you* with your kids.

PART 3

No Regrets Parenting
Your Adult Children

A Quick Review

*B*efore moving on to what *No Regrets Parenting* looks like after your kids finish high school and are ready for the next step, let's review your accomplishments to date. You have spent the past eighteen years conducting an intense preparatory class for life. It began in the delivery room, perhaps even in the womb, when your baby first felt your love. As your child grew, she felt your love grow as well, and she learned to love you back. At a certain very young age, your baby also began to observe your behavior; as she grew, she became more and more conscious of who you are, how you act, and what you believe. Soon, your little girl could ask questions, and she did, nonstop. And you diligently taught her, not only by your answers but also by your patience and honesty. When you were wrong, you admitted it and apologized. Because you were there for her, practicing *No Regrets Parenting*, capturing the moments that would otherwise have been lost to "efficiency," she learned to trust you. And as she grew into her teen years, the trust she learned from you paid off—you realized you could trust her, too.

All along, you set limits. From the first time you gently tucked your baby into her crib to the curfew you enforced on your driving teens, you provided the structure and set the limits every child needs. With this structure, and by your own role-modeling, you taught your kids right from wrong. Yet, you never lost sight of their need to grow their independence. As they grew, you gave them space. When their bedroom door was closed, you knocked. While never completely lowering your antennae, you kept a respectful distance when they were with friends. By balancing limits with liberty, you taught them respect—you for them, and they for you. And you gave your kids a road map for adult behavior.

Love, trust, and respect. Those are your accomplishments as a *no regrets* parent.

Now comes the hard part. And the fun part. It's time to see how the prototype young adult you molded in your home functions on his own. How well does the mutual *love, trust,* and *respect* you nurtured during his eighteen life-preparatory years hold up under the pressures of young adulthood? And as for you, how do you negotiate a path that allows you to continue to be a part of his life without regressing into pre-graduation parenting patterns, reversing all that you and he accomplished to get him here? This is THE moment when he should be putting all you taught him into practice. You mustn't take that moment away from him, or from you.

But first, what does "young adulthood" really mean?

The Developmental Milestones
of Young Adulthood

Well, we've talked about the developmental milestones of childhood and of parenthood, but there are also important developmental milestones of young adulthood which parents need to recognize.

As you read in "940 Saturdays and the 'Other' Biological Clock" in Part 1, many days raising your young children felt like they would never end, yet the years flew by fast, and suddenly your precious newborn is saying goodbye to you in her new dorm room or starting her new job and moving to her own apartment. Now what? What happens after kids leave home as young adults? Or what happens if they *don't* leave home and instead move into your basement?! Of course you're still their parents, and you still have parenting roles and responsibilities, but those have changed—they must change.

When does adulthood really begin? As when they were young, some adult kids mature faster than others and, as a *no regrets* parent, only you know how ready your kids are for adult responsibilities—but your kids will certainly have their own ideas about their readiness. And only you know when you're ready to give up many of the parenting practices you've observed in the past—but, again, be prepared that your kids will have other ideas for when it's time for you to back off. As a pediatrician, I have my own definition of young adulthood and, as with the stages of a young child's life, it is based on developmental milestones. One of the great wonders of childhood is its unpredictability. Kids will surprise you, and surprise their pediatricians like me, with their unique progress through the developmental milestones. Young kids have a way of finding their own pace and following the beat of their own drummer. Ditto your adult kids—there are significant differences among adult kids of the same age. But, for purposes of our discussion, I suggest that young adulthood begins when your child *begins* achieving these milestones which often, but not always, occur sequentially:

POST-HIGH SCHOOL EDUCATION—This may be college, trade school, or an apprenticeship, but it's a conscious step your child takes toward expanding their career options in life.

FIRST REAL JOB—This is not the after-school-earn-pocket-money job. This is the job with real responsibility, a real paycheck, and the potential for advancement.

FIRST HOME—This needn't be a purchased condo or house—a rented apartment, perhaps shared with a friend, counts here.

FIRST SIGNIFICANT RELATIONSHIP—A relationship with some-one who *could be* a long-term or lifetime partner.

FINANCIAL INDEPENDENCE—This doesn't mean *total* independence—young adults starting out may well need your ongoing support, but parental check-writing should begin decreasing in a meaningful way.

MARRIAGE—This is the *big one* and the single developmental milestone that *most* affects a parent's role with an adult child; more about this in "The Canopy. Really" chapter later.

CHILDREN—This also deserves its own discussion—see Part 4, *"No Regrets* Grand*parenting."*

How many milestones qualify as "young adulthood?" Just one! When your child has reached any one of those milestones, it's time to prepare for launch—and time to grow up with your children.

Growing Up with Your Children

This final pages of the book will, for some of you, feel like a distant mirage. If you still have young kids at home, picturing their post–high school years may seem wildly premature, and picturing your adult kids as parents themselves someday, well . . . impossible! But much as you've started saving money for your kids should they choose to continue their educations beyond high school, so you should also begin to think about building strategies for your relationships with your someday-soon-to-be young adult children. And if your kids are already on their way out the door, use these next chapters as a blueprint for maintaining the wonderful bonds you have worked so hard to create. You began building the fundamentals of these relationships while your kids were still in diapers; by the time they earned their driver's licenses, you were almost ready. *Almost.* Because nothing can quite prepare you for THE moment.

The previous chapters on principles and strategies of *No Regrets Parenting* help you capture the precious moments while your kids are young, anticipating THE moment. THE moment when you're standing at their new dorm room or apartment, or packing the car on your driveway, setting them "free" for college or their other young adult pursuits. THE moment may be one you've been dreading, or one you've been eagerly anticipating; either way, it's likely to be a moment filled with immense pride, nostalgia, and perhaps melancholy. But if you've been successful in your *No Regrets Parenting*, it will *not* be a moment of remorse or disappointment.

But now that THE moment has arrived and your kids are moving into the next very exciting phase of their lives, it's time for you to grow up with them and move into this next very exciting phase of *your* life. The goal of turning scarce minutes into cherished moments with your kids now becomes more challenging than ever and comes with a twist. As the nest empties and the complex choreography of having kids at home ebbs, you may find yourself with more time on your hands than you've been accustomed to for years. You're not rushing from work to catch their basketball game, or adjusting your morning schedule to drive car pool. But now it's your kids' minutes that are scarce—they have jam-packed class or work schedules, busy social lives, growing responsibilities.

Nature helps you make this transition gradually—as your kids grow from infants, to toddlers, to "middle-age" children, to tweens, and finally to adolescents, they progressively and appropriately separate themselves from your schedule. You read in the earlier parts of this book about recognizing and welcoming those biological changes as new opportunities to share precious moments with your kids. You learned strategies for accommodating your kids' growth by reprogramming your time accordingly. The biggest change in your agenda with your kids undoubtedly occurred when they began driving on their own— your chauffeuring skill was one of the last tethers you had to your teens; when your kids no longer need a ride, the countdown to liftoff begins. It is likely that you spent more quality time in a *week* with your seven-year-old than in a *year* with your seventeen-year-old. That's both normal and good. It prepares both you and your seventeen-year-old for the following year.

But the "following year" has now arrived, and it's time to again reprogram your time accordingly. Those projects you've been putting off, new interests you would like to explore, trips you've been dreaming about, the book you've always wanted to write—those are all on the immediate horizon. But first, you must successfully launch your adult kids into *their* new lives.

The keys to successfully making this next exciting transition in your life, and in your relationship with your kids, are *preparation* and *participation*.

Preparation for Launch

Not all kids leave home for college or jobs immediately after high school graduation, so the time to work out the logistics of the move may range from weeks to, well, years! Yes, it's true that while some kids only move as far as the basement of your home after high school, even they will seek higher ground eventually. The time between high school and moving on to college or a job is a whirlwind of logistical and practical to-do lists for you and your kids. Helping them shop for clothes, linens, and laptops; packing and shipping; booking transportation; farewell get-togethers with friends and family. Add to that your work and their summer job schedules to complicate the moments before they leave. But make time for one additional and very important item on your to-do list: create an actual "Launch List" to prepare your kids for what they should expect in college or out in the real world and *what you expect of them* . . .

Don't assume that all systems are go just because you've been preparing them for liftoff for eighteen years. Kids leave home at variable stages of readiness and maturity. It's unlikely, for example, that any high school graduate has had experience with a class schedule where some days don't start till noon, other days may have only two classes, and still others have nighttime lectures, labs, or study groups. Nor has high school prepared them for a rigorous work schedule where there's no one to shout up the stairs that they'll be late if they don't get out of bed *RIGHT NOW*! It's doubtful that your kids' high school experiences adequately prepared them for dorm life, cafeteria dining choices, or sorority pledging. Ditto job applications, apartment sharing, shopping and cooking for themselves, or commuting to work. While it is unfortunately true that many kids in high school have seen friends drink or do drugs, and that sex among high schoolers is not rare, the level of all of those exposures will rise to a new logarithmic scale in college and the real world.

It's not enough to kiss your kids goodbye and whisper in their ear, "Use your head; we trust you to do what's right; we respect your choices; we love you." Schedule a meeting with your new graduate before she takes the next step. Do it formally, sitting down with a cup of tea or bottle of soda and with the "Launch List." This is your compilation of all the things you can think of to tell them before they leave, no matter how many times you've told them the same things over the past eighteen years. Write them down, edit them, practice them, and then meticulously and patiently present them to your young astronaut. Don't cut corners—if it was important enough to put on the Launch List, it's important enough to tell your child (no matter how much they roll their eyes).

Talk about uncomfortable subjects; make them squirm a little ("Mommmm! C'mon, I know all that!") or a lot. Of course, they won't remember every word you say about dormitory and apartment fire escapes, or which foods are healthy, or setting two alarm clocks on test or work mornings, but they will remember the biggies—maybe because those are the ones that make them squirm the most. This is the ultimate in *no regrets* quality time with your child—it is *your* graduation speech to them as you transition from being the parent of a child to being the parent of a young adult.

More than ever, you now need to carve out special moments with your child before his liftoff. Set aside at least a couple hours, maybe in two sittings, and cover every topic on your list until you feel comfortable that he's heard what he needs to hear from you. Make sure it's not a one-way conversation. Ask him if he understands what you're saying and why you're saying it. Tell him about your own experiences that color your perspective and about news stories you've read or anecdotes you've heard that scare you about life "outside." This is one of the most important parenting opportunities you will have for a long time. It becomes much harder to be intimately involved in your kids' lives once they are out the door (but, as you'll read in the upcoming chapters, not impossible!). By the time they leave, you should have *no regrets* that you missed this chance for parting words and for imparting wisdom.

Here are a few ideas to get you started on your Launch List:

ACTIVITIES—balance your time carefully; school or work is your priority.

ALARM CLOCK—get to class or work on time; set two alarms.

ASSIGNMENT BOOK/CALENDAR—record every assignment and meeting.

CALL HOME—walking to class or to the subway for work, whenever you have a few minutes just to catch up; call your siblings often.

CIGARETTES—don't start; many lifelong smoking habits started in college or on lunch breaks at work.

CLOTHES/LAUNDRY—once a week is a good routine.

CULTURE—continue to grow and expand your horizons; go to exhibits, plays, and programs out of your comfort zone; take classes outside your major.

DIGITAL DISTRACTIONS—You're now in charge of your screen time; don't let it interfere with what's important.

DIVERSITY—be friends with people from as many different backgrounds as possible.

DRINKING—you know the drill, but I have to tell you again because it's important.

DRINKING 2—never walk away from your drink; if you do, don't drink it—get a new one.

DRUGS—you know the drill, but I have to tell you again because it's important.

EXERCISE—at least three times a week for physical *and* mental health.

FIRE HAZARDS/FIRE ESCAPES/FIRE EXTINGUISHERS—find them on day one.

FOOD—foods that were healthy at home are still healthy.

FRIENDS—pick them carefully; avoid people who are trouble—you know who they are.

GROOMING—you only get one chance to make a first impression.

HEALTH—sleep enough, eat right, exercise, wash your hands frequently. Be comfortable getting checked out by a doctor if you're worried about something.

HOMESICK—it happens to everyone; call home, video chat with us, let us help.

MAIL—we'll be sending surprise care bundles, so check your mail often.

MEDICINE—don't share your medicine with others or take anyone else's.

MONEY—make wise choices; cut corners where you can.

MOOD—be sensitive to your mood; if you're feeling depressed or sad, tell us or your doctor right away.

ORGANIZE—your desk, your apartment, your clothes drawers; no one's picking up after you.

SECURITY/SAFETY—lock your door when you're out; try not to walk alone at night.

SEX—you know the drill, but I have to tell you again because it's important.

SLEEP—you need at least eight hours a night to learn and work effectively and to stay healthy.

TRAVEL/ROAD TRIPS—let us know about travel you are planning.

VISITS—we would love to visit as often as we can, but only if the timing is right for you; if you need us urgently, tell us right away and we'll be there.

WEATHER—dress for the weather; cold and gray can be depressing; tell us if you are sad.

Then, after you've gone through every item on your list, it's *now* time to give your child a hug and a kiss, and whisper in his ear, "Use your head; we trust you to do what's right; we respect your choices; we love you."

Participation—Staying Close with Your Adult Kids

*P*arenting doesn't end after Saturday #940; kids still have big issues and, in some ways, need your wisdom and experience even more than when they were in high school. But staying close with your young adult children now depends much more on their schedules than on yours. You may well find yourself with more time on your hands just when your kids have less time for you. That's as it should be. Despite your best efforts to get together, you're without your adult children most of the time, and you understand well what the American novelist Christopher Morley meant when he said, "We've had bad luck with our kids . . . they've all grown up."

Of course, children must move on with their lives, so here are a few ideas that can help you with the transition while still participating in your kids' futures:

1. As you read in the "Calendars" section of this book for your younger kids, if your adult kids are continuing their education, at the start of each academic year record their school calendars in your home calendar, scouring for overlapping free days that may allow visits for you or them. R.S.V.P. "no" to commitments that conflict with your kids' vacations or with Parents' Weekend in case you're able to sneak in a visit.

2. When a professional meeting, work travel, or a family occasion puts you in a city near your child, visit her on campus or at her apartment for a quick lunch or dinner.

3. Continue to practice the delayed gratification you mastered when they were little. Spend your vacation days, vacation dollars, and frequent-flier miles on getting to your children and getting them to you.

4. Welcome "microbursts" of communication. Encourage your kids to call or text during their walks between classes or on their way home from work. Not every day, but maybe once a week. This keeps you in touch with the developments in their lives and gives you a chance to celebrate or commiserate about the big game last week.

5. As you read in the "Homework Helper" chapter earlier, when your children are growing up, it's a good idea to periodically check on their homework to make sure they are on track. It's still a good idea when they're young adults, but now for a different reason. If they are in school, ask them to send you papers they've written and are particularly proud of, or to recommend books they enjoyed reading for class so you can keep up with what they're learning and thinking. If your kids are in the workforce, ask them to share project summaries or reports they submitted to their bosses and performance evaluations they've earned. These steps keep you in the loop of their lives.

6. FaceTime, Zoom, Google Meet, Skype, and other virtual visits are wondrous for getting through the birthdays, holidays, and other milestones you miss when your kids

aren't home. You can get virtual tours of their dorms, apartments, and workplaces, and they get to see you, their grandparents, and the dog they left back home.

7. If you have more than one adult child, make a "rule" (you're still the parents!) that the kids should touch base with one another, preferably by phone rather than just texting or Facebook, at least once a week. And subtly check up to see that it's happening. You'll find, as you and your kids get older, that the relationship they have with each other becomes more gratifying and comforting to you than even their relationship with you. Adult siblings often have even more to offer each other than you have to offer them. Simple geometry applies here—their lives are now parallel whereas your life and your kids' lives are perpendicular.

8. Limp your way through Facebook, Twitter, and Instagram to catch the glimpses of their school and work lives they post online. Hopefully you'll remain "friends," not only on social media but in real life, too.

9. Finally, don't panic if the contact you have with your kids becomes less frequent than you'd like. They need space to test their wings. You'll reach a new equilibrium with them, and all the lessons you taught them as a *no regrets* parent when they were younger will gradually percolate through and resonate with them—and then they'll call more often.

Now that we've strategized how to prepare for, and participate in, your kids' young adulthoods, the next critically important step is to establish boundaries.

Boundaries

F or your child to successfully launch, you'll soon need to be able (and willing!) to detach your booster rocket from her spaceship, so it's time to redefine your parenting boundaries (or, I guess if I was to stick with the spaceship metaphor, your parenting *coordinates* ☺). Of course, as when they were younger, you would do just about anything for your adult kids because your dreams for them are boundless—health, happiness, success. You hope they avoid life's pitfalls yet show resilience when they inevitably stumble; learn both from your mistakes and from your accomplishments; and grow to be kind and meaningful contributors to a better world. You wish them a life at least as good if not better than your own. Although your dreams for them are *boundless*, your relationships with them must have *boundaries*. Most importantly, boundaries are your best strategy for the overarching goal of *No Regrets Parenting*—turning *minutes* into meaningful *moments* with your kids, now your adult kids. Without boundaries, you risk distancing them and losing those moments.

From crib to canopy and beyond, you have manifold opportunities to cheer, steer, prepare, and protect your children. Yet, as when they were younger, adult kids need to learn from their own mistakes to grow and mature. The dilemma for parents of adult kids is that the consequences of their mistakes are so much greater than the consequences of the mistakes they made in young childhood. Jobs, homes, financial futures, marriages, and children are at stake when adult kids make mistakes. My wife and I often joke about the "rotation" in our worry list—our three adult kids seem to take turns topping the list of causes for our sleepless nights. Yet, as much as we would like to try fixing all of our adult kids' problems as we tried when they were younger, we can't and we shouldn't. Even when they were younger, the balance between fixing kids' mistakes and letting them learn from them was always a challenge. Now, with adult kids, it's even more important to respect boundaries and let your young adult kids learn from their mistakes as you did when you were young adults.

So . . . here are my *No Regrets Parenting* recommendations for respecting boundaries with your adult kids:

> **GIVING ADVICE.** After you've spent time reviewing the "Launch List" (see previous chapter "Preparation for Launch"), your parenting advice "magnus opus," now you should wait for your kids to ask for your advice as they embark on their young adult voyage. But they probably won't. Be very selective about when you give advice—most situations your child finds himself in are best handled by your child without your advice; that's how he learns. But when you see a situation that you feel requires your advice, because the risks of your child's actions or of a bad decision are high, advise gently. Use examples from your own young adulthood or those of friends and family members your children may know. Describe the best-case scenarios of their decisions before projecting the worst-case scenarios. Carrots work better than sticks in guiding children of all ages. If your child is married, give your advice privately to your child, not in front of their partner— uninvited advice to an in-law child risks alienating your child and their spouse, putting both in an awkward position. Your child can then decide whether to pass along your message. And it's best to speak in person or by phone rather than with email or text messages that may be misinterpreted by your

child or seen by their partner—this is not meant to be sneaky, only respectful of their marriage and the boundaries it requires (see "The Canopy. Really" upcoming chapter). In-law children are rarely fond of intervention by their spouse's parents— "invasive" and "intrusive" are the words that most often come to your in-law child's mind.

If you give your advice and your child accepts and appreciates it, great! If she thanks you but says she'll figure it out, don't pursue it. As painful as lessons from life's hard knocks can be, we've all had them, and they are formative. And, of course, there's never a place for "I told you so."

GETTING TOGETHER. If your child lives locally on their own, don't show up uninvited. Invite your adult kids to your home for special occasions or just for short visits and home cooking—but don't pressure them or make them feel guilty when they turn you down. And it's okay if they don't invite you to their place very often—that's part of the necessary separation process (and helps them conceal the dirty dishes and stacks of laundry from you). You'll probably hear from them when there's a leaky faucet or when the pilot light on the furnace goes out, so make the most of those moments and use them to casually learn what's going on in their lives.

If your child isn't local, plan your visits around *their* school or work schedules. The decision of whether or not to stay at their place when you visit is very personal—for some adult kids, having you stay with them is a fun way to show off their independence; for others, it's anathema. Only you and your kids can determine which it is.

CALLING. Calls to your adult child should also respect their schedules—don't interrupt their class, work, travel, or family time. This requires some knowledge of their commitments, which also needs to be gathered thoughtfully—when you're together with your adult kids for dinners or family gatherings (or to fix the leaky faucet), catch up on their lives while making mental notes of good and bad times to connect. If you're fortunate enough that your kids call you with some frequency, wait for their calls—that way you know it's a convenient time for them.

SHARING. Cherish what your adult kids share with you about their lives, but don't pry. Ask general questions, and expect the same one- or two-word answers you got when they were little: What's new? ("Not much.") How are your classes? ("Good.") How's work? ("Good.") How's your wife's (husband's) school, work, family? ("All good.") Your kids may or may not confide in you about important times and issues in their lives, but this shouldn't be like the question-and-answer I described in the earlier chapter on "The Daily Dinner Meeting"; hopefully those sessions when your kids were younger created muscle memory about giving more than one-word answers. But even if not, your adult kids have earned their privacy, and it should be respected.

If you feel your adult kids aren't sharing enough about their lives to make you feel a part of them, schedule lunch or coffee at their convenience. It's okay to gently tell them you're going through a bit of withdrawal and would love to be more involved and aware of what's going on with them. And in exchange, you'll buy lunch. ☺

GIFTS AND MONEY. When your kids were little, you stressed a bit over the best gifts to give them for special occasions, but because you are a *no regrets* parent, you had a really good idea of which toy or bike or game would give them the biggest smile. And you may well have the same radar for your adult kids, but their greatest wishes and wants are those they now know best. "What would you like for your birthday this year?" is a great question to ask, and you may get a great answer that you're happy to abide. But, although the least creative of gifts, cash is often the most appreciated. This is not to say that special, personal gifts aren't valued and shouldn't be given. Of course they should. Gift cards or certificates to their favorite store? Okay, but cash accomplishes the same goal and gives them the flexibility to use it in their second favorite store this time— or to put it toward their rent or mortgage. And they're less likely to lose cash than a gift certificate. The exception to this suggestion is if you feel your kids are poor managers of money and that giving them more of it would be enabling them rather than facilitating their thoughtful approach to budgeting. In that case, a nice sweater or jacket is probably a better idea.

THE CANOPY—Your kids' marriage is the most significant factor in redefining boundaries with your adult kids, and it deserves its own chapter (to follow).

CROSSING BOUNDARIES—There are times when, as the parent of an adult child, you must cross a boundary. These are emergent situations, and forcibly or aggressively violating a boundary should never be undertaken lightly. Here are a few examples of when you must:

- Addiction
- Infidelity
- Criminal activity
- Bankruptcy
- Domestic abuse

In these rare instances, your most important intervention is to get professional help for your adult child. Your personal involvement, rather than the guidance a professional can give your child, may do more harm than good—your child may resent your intervention and withdraw entirely from you, and the advice you give may be the wrong advice.

The Canopy. Really

Nothing prepares you adequately for your child's wedding, so expect to be overwhelmed and, if all goes well, overjoyed. Your child's marriage completely redefines your relationship with her because now there's someone else in her life who must take priority over you. That's as it should be.

Let's start with the wedding itself. Planning the ceremony with all its trappings can be the most fulfilling, or the most frustrating, process of parenting your adult child. It's important to restate our goal here—you want to remain a meaningful part of your child's life well beyond the ceremony with many more *No Regrets Parenting* moments. The most significant regret to avoid at all costs (and costs are a very significant factor; see below!) is hard feelings about the ceremony that distance your child from you. It's your child's wedding and, unless he tells you otherwise, your involvement in the planning of the event should be helpful and supportive, but not invasive or meddlesome.

Unless the happy couple elopes, the riskiest wedding issue for maintenance of your relationship with your child and their partner is the cost of the wedding. If they offer to plan the wedding, and they usually will offer to plan or at least help with planning the major details and guest list, let them—but establish early on who is paying for what. If you've been practicing *No Regrets Parenting* all along, this will not be as treacherous a discussion as you might think. Your child has seen you make wise financial decisions and has learned from the budgeting you have demonstrated and the sacrifices you have made (see "Money" in Part 1). The "small businesses" you helped them start (see "Making Lemonade—Their Office (and Allowances)" in Part 2), the generosity you taught them (see "Charity Starts in the Home" in Part 2), and the hard work you showed them you do (see "A Corner (of Your) Office" in Part 2) have all prepared your kids for this most grownup of all financial discussions: paying for the wedding. This is a very individualized process, requiring participation by all parties—a grownup version of the "Shareholder Meetings" described in Part 2. There is no one-size-fits-all solution as there might have been generations ago when, by tradition, the bride's family bore the brunt of the expense—unless that's what everyone agrees on. Rather, your child and her spouse, her spouse's parents (see "The Happy Couple" chapter to follow), and you will all likely make contributions to the cost, but foremost in the discussion must be your child's happiness with the plan. Work closely and warmly and candidly with your child and her spouse to get there.

The wedding day itself can feel chaotic, and it goes by so quickly that you may find yourself looking at the photo album months later to recall everything that happened. But the ceremony is another wonderful opportunity for really *seeing* a monumental milestone in your child's life. As when they were younger, try "The Parenting Meditation" (Part 1) to really be in this moment in your child's life. And, as I wrote in that chapter, what works for me to help drown out some of the din and lock in the memories at important times like this is "channeling" a loved one who couldn't be at the wedding.

Oh, and by the way, don't expect to have time to eat the delicious meal you helped plan and pay for!

The Happy Couple

Now that the ceremony is over and your "little one" is married, it's time to address your role in the rest of your married child's life! The most important realization for you now is that even though your child is still at the top of your priority list (see "Who Are You?" in the Introduction), you are *not* the top priority on your child's list. That's worth repeating—you are *not* the top priority on your child's list; their spouse must be. And you must now shift from a starring role in your child's life to a supporting cast member, and that's not easy for a *no regrets* parent who has been intimately involved since the crib. Time to back off, Mom! Chillax, Dad!

And then it gets even more complicated. Although your child's happiness will always be a top priority for you, the only way you can guarantee happiness is by supporting their marriage—everything you do as a parent going forward must respect the sanctity of your child's marriage and the transcendence of the couple. That means you should never find yourself "siding" with your child over their spouse. One of the worst parenting mistakes you can make with your married child is speaking negatively about, or advocating against, their spouse. An in-law parent's actions and words can drive a wedge in your relationship with your child who must first and foremost be their spouse's unwavering advocate. That doesn't mean your child abandons you or doesn't speak on your behalf to their spouse when there's a brewing problem—but that must be on your child's initiative, not because you asked them to. For the sake of the couple, keep anything but loving and positive opinions to yourself.

To further complicate things, your child's spouse has their own family! Ideally, your relationship with your in-law child's family will be a warm one, but anything less than that is another potential landmine in your quest for a *no regrets* relationship with your adult child. Among their top priorities must be a loving and respectful relationship with their in-law parents, and anything you do to undermine that relationship will undermine your relationship with your child. Again, unless you have positive things to say about your child's in-laws, keep quiet. Better yet, *find* reasons to have positive things to say about them. Initiate contact with the in-laws, calling on holidays and special occasions, thanking them for raising such a wonderful spouse or partner for your child, and bragging together about the young couple. This friendship may at first seem contrived— after all, you probably didn't even know the in-laws before your child and their spouse met, and you didn't choose the in-laws as friends. But now, they must become among your most important friends—for the sake of the young couple.

Finally, the boundaries you establish between you and your adult child, as detailed two chapters back, must be even more strictly adhered to once he is married. Rarely give unsolicited advice: coordinate all visits and calls with the couple's schedule; cherish the details of their lives they share with you, but don't pry; on special occasions, ask the couple what the most meaningful and helpful gifts would be. The key words for your relationship with your married child and their spouse are "helpful" and "supportive"—but don't force your help on them. Let the couple know you're available whenever they need, and then leave it to them to call on you rather than bombarding them with offers to help. Don't make the couple feel guilty for saying, "No, thanks, we're good."

The very rare occasions when you might have to cross boundaries are the same as in the earlier chapter—but your threshold for doing so must be even higher when a spouse is involved; hopefully you'll never reach that threshold.

The adjustments to having a married child are profound, but you should welcome this opportunity for your ongoing evolution as a seasoned adult. As you read in "Growing Up with Your Children" a few chapters back, now it's your time to tackle all the projects you put off, explore new interests, and maybe even slow down a bit. But you want the happy couple to remain an important part of your life, so please don't ever feel, "They're out the door; they don't really need me to be involved anymore." By your actions and words, your married kids should know you want to be involved and included in their lives, but on their schedules and at their bidding.

Now, it might be time for grandchildren (Part 4)!

Congratulations!

You've done it! They're in college or out in the world!

You have raised wonderful children who love their parents and *know* their parents. You turned countless childhood minutes, hours, days, and weeks that would have otherwise been lost in the name of expediency into special moments you'll cherish forever. You were there with them every chance you had, and you created chances to be with them you never imagined you could.

And as a reward for your commitment, passion, and love, you can now pass by their empty bedrooms, feeling fond nostalgia and missing them terribly. But what a blessing it is to feel *no regrets*!

The days were long, the years were short, and the time you had with them was then. But you made the time, and you took the time.

Now it's your time. You earned it.

PART 4

No Regrets
Grandparenting

Preface for Parents: Helping Your Parents Transition to Being Grandparents

*M*uch as becoming a parent was a huge development in your life, becoming a grandparent is a huge development in your own parents' lives. Helping them through this milestone can make them more sensitive to your needs and expectations as a parent.

First, take a moment for grandparent appreciation. Now that you have firsthand experience with parenting young kids, give your parents a shout-out for all the effort, energy, and love they showed raising you. Next, recognize that your parents, the new grandparents, may be a little lost. After finally finding their rhythm as parents and even reluctantly accepting the fact that their kids are adults, their first instinct as grandparents is probably . . . to parent! They can't help it; they've been doing it for so long, evolving along the way through the Developmental Milestones of Parenthood (see Part 1). Also, realize that your parents love your children with a love few others will ever feel for them. Grandparents make mistakes, usually not intentionally or maliciously—they're new at this and you need to guide them. Having loving grandparents involved in your kids' lives is an invaluable blessing, and you should do everything in your power to nurture that relationship—without undermining the family dynamic you are committed to establishing. It's your family now and, if it's at all possible, having your parents as a meaningful part of it should be the goal.

Here are a few suggestions to help your parents with their transition to grandparenthood.

1. **BE PATIENT.** Your parents are going through growing pains. Much like the disorientation and apprehension you've experienced as new parents, your parents are now experiencing the "bends" as grandparents. They love you and your kids but may struggle to find the right ways to show it. They may over-gift, over-feed, over-hug-and-kiss, over-protect, over-worry, over-lecture, and in general overstep their new roles. It will pass. Probably. But you can help it pass by having a constructive conversation with your parents or in-laws about mutual respect. Tell them that respecting your rules for your kids is critical for your relationship with your parents or in-laws and that it's now your turn to parent and try to do the wonderful job they did when you and your partner were young. And if they didn't do such a wonderful job, be gentle about pointing that out, but be firm in telling them what they should not do with your children that they may have done with you. This is about boundaries (and refer them to the upcoming chapter, "Boundaries, Again!").

2. **LISTEN TO THEIR ADVICE . . . AND THEN FILTER IT.** It's natural for your parents to offer suggestions about childrearing and parenting—they've been doing it a lot longer than you and it's become a reflex. Listen to what they have to say, but then pick and choose which advice to accept and which to ignore. Your parents won't be (too) offended about the ignored advice; it's important for them to know you heard them, but deep down, they really do know that it's your job to be the decider now. Just saying their piece is usually enough for grandparents to move on to the next lesson. There are also instructions for your parents regarding advice they should *never* give you—you can show that list to them in same upcoming "Boundaries, Again!" chapter.

3. **BE POLITE AND COMMUNICATE EFFECTIVELY.** There are nice ways and not-so-nice ways of telling your parents they're being invasive or intrusive. Choose the nice ways. You might say, "Mom, we have decided to try it a different way with Tyler than the way you and Dad chose with us as kids, but knowing how you did it gives us a great backup plan." That will send the same message as, "You had your turn; now it's our turn, so back off," but in a kinder and more respectful way. Make your rules for your kids clear to your parents; you are the parent, and you are happy to have your parents spend time and have special moments with your children—but your rules rule. These include rules about discipline, bedtime, snacks, outings, activities, etc. I spell these out for your parents in the upcoming "Activities" chapter.

4. **DON'T BE TOO PROUD.** Occasionally, let yourself ask for your parents' advice, especially when you can really use it. Soliciting their help on your terms will show them that you value their opinions, and it will also subtly show them that when you do need advice, you'll ask for it (so if you don't ask, it means you don't need it). Asking for your parents' help isn't an admission of failure as a parent or a sign of weakness—it's being honest about your evolution as a parent and your respect for the people who have already gone through it.

5. **SHARE AND INCLUDE (BUT DON'T OVERSHARE).** The toughest thing for grandparents to adjust to is having only a part-time role in your kids' lives. When there are events at your kids' preschool, or a nearby soccer or T-ball game, invite the grandparents. Not necessarily every

time, but often enough to help them feel like they're part of their grandkids' fun experiences. It's a painless visit for you with your parents, and there's a natural endpoint when the event is over. If you live far from your parents, schedule regular video visits so your kids don't change so much between in-person visits that your parents feel the distance even more acutely. Send pictures by email and text, or teach your parents how to follow you on Instagram—grandparents live for those small gestures from you and the digital mementos they can use to brag to their friends. Sharing is different from *oversharing*. Your parents don't need to know every, or even most details of your kids' lives—just share enough for your parents to feel they have a meaningful place in, and a good view of, their grandkids' childhoods. Too much sharing can lead to grandparents feeling entitled to be involved in your decisions and rules. In particular, avoid sharing things which you already know, or strongly suspect, you and your parents disagree on—that leads to unnecessary conflict.

6. **BE FORGIVING, AND AVOID PUNISHING YOUR PARENTS.** Inevitably, and hopefully unintentionally, your parents will say or do things that are insensitive and hurt your feelings. Gently explain to them what it is they did wrong and the effect it had on you and/or on your kids. Ask them to be more thoughtful about the impact of their words and deeds in the future. But also give them the benefit of the doubt and realize they mean well and have your and your kids' well-being at heart. Punishing your parents by limiting their access to their grandchildren should be an absolute last resort.

7. **FINALLY, HAND THIS BOOK YOUR PARENTS.** And tell them to start with Part 4.

Congratulations, Again!
You're a Grandparent!

What?? You're a grandparent? You're much too young for that! Well now, congratulations are REALLY in order! Not only have you "graduated" from parenting young kids, but now you have a chance to relive the joy of a new baby and the wondrous developments that follow!

Grandparents are special people in a family's life, and their roles in their families are as varied as their backgrounds and life experiences. From seeing grandchildren only over video chat or in person on occasional weekends, to actually raising grandchildren because of difficult family situations, grandparents should also be able to feel *no regrets*. But, despite the great joy grandparenting can bring, it *can* cause regrets. I hope to help you navigate the thrilling, sometimes treacherous, grandparenting experience, leaving you with *no regrets*.

Since the first edition of this book, Sara and I have become grandparents, and it's SO different from becoming parents. Watching our son become a father was like nothing I had ever experienced in my life. Of course, I felt great joy and wonder at the births of our kids, but so much of those early days with young kids is blurred by the worry, uncertainty, and choreography that comes with new parenthood. But with the sanguinity and calm of being able to step back, watch our son experience with his son what we experienced with him, and leave the diapering to the new mother and father, I was able to again truly appreciate the miracle of new life and take in every precious minute spent with my new grandchild. Indeed, as the title of this book says, every *minute* with grandchildren can become a *moment* to cherish.

That said, grandparents can have worry and uncertainty, too— not just about their grandchildren, but about their adult children who have become new parents. How do grandchildren change your relationship with your child? In the following brief chapters, I share a road map for grandparents and, as I wrote in the Introduction, for young parents who are hoping to tactfully guide their own parents through the grandparenting experience.

First, we need to establish yet another set of boundaries.

Boundaries, Again!

*E*verything you read a few chapters back on the boundaries to respect with your young adult kids, and with their spouses or partners, applies to grandparenting, but *on steroids!* Boundaries for giving advice, getting together, calling, sharing, and gifts become all the more important when your kids' *kids* are involved. It's not so much because your grandkids want you to respect boundaries—they'd be happy to be totally spoiled by their loving grandparents—but because your adult kids, now parents themselves, deserve and will demand new boundaries even stricter than the ones you established together when they became young adults. If your kids have a partner in their child raising, their partner will also rightfully expect—and help set—grandparent boundaries. First and foremost, don't disrespect the parents of your grandchildren. They are the rule makers, the child raisers, and the gatekeepers.

Let's revisit the boundaries between parents and young adults, now with an eye toward the grandchildren and their parents.

GIVING ADVICE

You probably feel that your experience raising your kids should qualify you as a welcome resource for your child and their partner in raising your grandchildren. Wrong. You may be qualified, but your advice will likely not be welcome—at least, not as welcome as you would like. Why? Because it's your kids' turn, and today's parents have so many resources other than you for guidance. As I wrote in an earlier chapter "The Checkered History of Parenting Advice" (see Part 1), parenting books abound, but who needs parenting books these days when online experts (and, unfortunately, non-experts) post daily wisdom? So, to get the *most* minutes and the *best* moments with grandkids, you must limit the advice you give their parents, lest they withdraw from you. Of course, if your adult children *ask* for your advice, give it freely and honestly and lovingly. But don't hold your breath waiting for them to ask.

And unless they ask, here are just a few things *not to give advice* about, because these are areas that are privileged parenting prerogatives where your advice is least likely to be welcome:

Names they plan to give their children. Number of children they're planning for. Food and feeding. Clothes. School. Discipline. Choice to work or stay home. Bedtime. Healthcare. Haircuts. Hygiene. Crying and temper tantrums. Manners. Potty training. After-school activities. Chores. Homework. Holidays. Family traditions. Screen time. Screen choices. Pets. Toys.

GETTING TOGETHER, CALLING, AND SHARING

Follow the rules in the earlier chapters for getting together with your young adult kids, but follow them all the more strictly now that there's a grandchild involved. If they are local, don't show up to their home uninvited. Invite your grandkids and your adult kids' family to your home when appropriate, but don't pressure them, and don't make them feel guilty when they turn you down. If your child isn't local, plan your visits around the family's schedule, and that includes your phone calls. Your calls should respect their schedules, and their schedules are so much more complicated now that they have a child. In addition to all the variables in your adult kids' schedules, you now need to be conscious about bedtimes, bath times, feeding/dinner hours, daycare/preschool hours. Best to wait for their calls or texts.

Cherish what your adult kids share with you about your grandchildren, but don't pry. Of course, it would be wonderful if they shared every new developmental milestone, all the cute things their little one says, and the sweet feedback from the preschool teacher about your grandkids, but don't be upset if you don't get those news flashes. Remember the frenzy of parenthood you felt when your kids were little? That's the frenzy going on in your grandchildren's home right now. Today's version of sharing might be the pictures your adult kids post on social media, so make sure you're "friends" with them on the sites they use (unless they ask you not to follow them—that type of discord requires special help). And when you do follow them, best not to add comments, or limit your comments to hearts and kisses emojis since everything you post may be seen by others and could embarrass your kids.

GIFTS AND MONEY

For a young and growing family, cash money may again be the most appreciated gift. But with grandkids, you'll be tempted to go overboard with gifts, toys, dolls, books, and clothes. Overboard should be avoided. Yes, grandparents are allowed to "spoil" their grandkids (unless their parents ask you not to), but use good sense because you're being judged by the gifts you give. Are there hidden messages you're trying to send with those gifts? "Educational" books, for example, can be interpreted by your grandkids' parents as a clue you think their kids aren't reading enough or learning their addition and subtraction fast enough. Will a baseball mitt or football jersey suggest to your kids that you want them to get your grandkids more involved in sports when they haven't shown an interest in them? Dolls and toy trucks can be tricky, too—respect your kids' social norms regarding gender-biased gifts. Most parents today would prefer that their kids not play with plastic guns or other weapon toys—even squirt guns, Nerf guns, bows and arrows, and soft darts are objectionable to many parents.

Unless their parents know in advance and approve, don't give your grandkids pets! And finally, don't give your grandkids gifts that will annoy their parents by being too noisy or too messy.

As with all aspects of parenting, grandparents who give the best gifts are those who know their grandkids the best. But no one knows their grandchildren as well as the grandchildren's parents—so ask them what they recommend for gifts. Some parents even establish a "registry" of gifts on Amazon or elsewhere to help clueless grandparents and others in advance of birthdays and holidays.

WHEN TO CROSS BOUNDARIES

The few (and extreme) examples given in the earlier chapter about when you should interject in your kids' lives without their permission certainly apply to them when they have their own kids, too. But grandkids add a few new situations that warrant crossing boundaries. Remember, your opportunity to spend meaningful *no regrets* time with your grandchildren is determined entirely by their parents, and crossing delicate boundaries could drive a wedge between you and your children and ultimately distance you from your grandchildren. That said, there are times when you must take that risk because the risk to your grandchildren if you *don't* intervene is greater.

Your grandkids' safety, of course, is paramount. If your kids aren't strapping your grandkids into car seats or using seat belts, you have to say something—but gently. Perhaps buying a car seat for them is the best approach. Bike helmets, childproofing (electric outlets, medicines, cleaning supplies, etc.), and dangerous street-crossing practices are other examples where finding a sensitive way to protect your grandchildren is appropriate.

Other areas of concern you might have about your grandchild's well-being require even more sensitivity before intervening. For example, if you believe your grandchild might be developmentally delayed, severely overweight or underweight, abused or neglected, bullied or bullying, his parents could very understandably be insulted by any suggestion of those possibilities from you. Yet, it's important to find a way to help your grandchild. These situations require special expertise, and you should discuss the best approaches in confidence, with a therapist, school counselor, clergy member, pediatrician, family physician, or teacher.

Finally, there are unfortunate circumstances where grandparents must take over raising their grandchildren. This can engender a wide range of deep emotions among the grandchildren, their parents, and the grandparents; the resulting challenges are manifold. Self-care and support systems become critically important for grandparents who are not prepared physically, emotionally, and/or financially. Of course, the grandchildren are not prepared, either. The eight essential requirements of all children, described in Part 1 ("What Do Your Kids Need from You?"), are now even more essential because one or more of these were likely missing in their previous home environment. Again, those essentials are: security, stability, consistency, emotional support, love, education, positive role models, and structure. When taking over as primary caregivers for grandchildren, it's important for grandparents to recognize that being deprived of any of their essential needs will harm their grandchildren in the short term and potentially scar them for much longer. But helping your grandchildren heal, and making their lives purposeful and successful, can bring you the greatest satisfaction you've ever known.

All of the fundamentals of *No Regrets Parenting* detailed in Part 1 of this book for parents apply to grandparents who are primary caregivers—but none more important than the chapters on "3D Parenting," "Listening," "Best Friend or Parent," and, as mentioned above, "What Do Your Kids Need from You?"

Activities

Because the time you have to enjoy your grandchildren in any given day or week is probably less than you would prefer, and certainly less than the time you had with your own young kids, making the most of your grandparenting time—by turning fleeting *minutes* into cherished *moments*—is all the more important. But an important word of caution: don't make your access to your grandkids an issue or source of conflict between you and your kids, and don't complain to them about not having enough time with your grandkids. Let your kids know you're available and love being with your grandkids, but your kids are, and must be, the gatekeepers of your access to your grandkids. Their family has schedules, choreography, and responsibilities just like your family did when your kids were young. Recognize that it's now your kids' turn to parent. Love every minute you're with your grandkids, and fill the time you're not with them doing things that you've always wanted to do but didn't have the time for. By being less insistent or aggressive in asking for time with your grandkids, your kids will feel less threatened, guilty, or imposed upon, and hopefully they'll give you more time, especially when the time you spend caring for your grandkids helps with the schedules, choreography, and responsibilities of their household. If this doesn't happen, sit down with your adult child for coffee or lunch (see previous "Boundaries" chapter in Part 3), and gently ask how you might squeeze out a little more time with your grandkids.

Next, face it—you're not as young as you used to be. If you *feel* as young as you used to, and you're physically able, that's wonderful,

272 NO REGRETS PARENTING

and all the activities described in the earlier chapters for parents and their kids still apply to you with your grandkids. A word of caution, though—even if you *feel* as young as you used to feel, self-care is even more important at your age than when you were a young parent. Refer to the earlier chapter on "Staying Sane" in Part 1 of this book for the mental tricks to coping with young kids, but add to those strategies your need to stay physically healthy and safe. Exercise caution in pushing yourself too hard—your grandkids can run, jump, skip, swim, and throw snowballs and baseballs and Frisbees with more energy than you, and their balance on bikes and hikes is probably better than yours. If you try to keep up with everything they're capable of doing, you risk limiting your years with them.

Before we get to the suggested activities with your grandchildren, here are a few things you should *never* do with them—because they're unsafe, unwise, or cross boundaries you shouldn't be crossing (see previous chapter). *Unless you have their parents' permission*, don't post your grandkids' pictures or stories about them on social media; let other people babysit them, even for a few minutes; take them for outings; give haircuts.

Also, don't do these: criticize their parents or other family members in front of your grandkids; disobey their parents' rules (bedtimes, discipline, potty training, screen time, clothes, snacks, medicines, manners, temper tantrums) or meddle in their parents' decisions; invite yourself to their activities; or ask your grandkids personal or private things about their parents. And, of course, don't show favorites among your grandchildren.

GENERAL PRINCIPLES

When playing with your grandchildren, here are a few general principles to follow:

1. Your grandkids' activities will make a big mess. Good. Messes show involvement, enthusiasm, and creativity. When the activity is over, depending on the ages of your grandchildren, clean-up time together is also good.

2. Often less is more—when kids have too many toys around them, it's harder for them to engage in focused activity. Focus is important for their maturation and evolution through childhood, and for bringing a little calm to your playdates.

3. Be conscious of the activities that best capture your grandkids' interests, and nurture them. Art? Music? Sports? Superheroes? Construction? Trains?

4. Be sparing with TV, video games, and other screen time (see so many previous chapters in this book!). Time with your grandchildren is precious, and it's a shame to waste it while they're zoned out in front of a screen. That said, watching or playing on screens with you can be a welcome way for them (and you!) to take a breather from all the other more physical forms of play. As with everything else having to do with your grandkids, check with their parents' for preferences and limitations on screen time.

Now for the fun stuff . . . For those of you who are of a certain age—and feeling your age—many of the activities which follow are a bit gentler and mellower, but they should be no less memorable if you keep in mind the strategies outlined in earlier chapters for turning minutes into moments. Disclaimer: I didn't compile these activities all on my own. As I mentioned earlier, Sara and I have become grandparents since the first edition of this book, and we are fortunate to have many friends and colleagues who have also reached that milestone in their lives. So . . . I reached out to dozens of fellow grandparents (see the Acknowledgments for the list) for their favorite activities with their grandchildren; the ages of their grandchildren ranged from newborn to young adult—and there was even one lucky grandma who has four *great-grandchildren!* What emerged from this little survey moved me greatly: an outpouring of unbridled and extraordinary love from grandparents for their grandchildren, and immense gratitude for the blessing of having their grandchildren be a part of their lives.

Perhaps most telling, these simple but heartfelt responses to the "What are your favorite activities with your grandchildren?" question were universal: snuggling, cuddling, holding, hugging, and . . . marveling. Sleepovers, with bedtimes and bath times, were especially cherished. Grandparents expressed sentiments like these: "I feel the utmost gratitude and love when they want to sit on my lap after a meal and just want to snuggle while the others continue to eat and chat," and "I like cuddling with them while we read together, or just cuddling while we do nothing."

In the "Parenting Meditation" chapter in Part 1, I suggested ways that parents might pause long enough to appreciate the little miracles they created, but even those brief pauses for parents to appreciate their kids are a challenge during the tumult of a busy household. Grandparents, on the other hand, have the luxury of stepping back and witnessing the wonder of childhood, as one grandmother so beautifully expressed: "I love just staring at them and marveling at their beauty, energy, laughter, and creativity." Hugging took all forms; a disabled but doting grandfather wrote, "I'm not able to stand and walk with them. But they have this almost innate understanding and will gingerly hug my legs when they run to me for a hug so as not to cause me to lose my balance. It is a wonder to watch how natural and accepting grandchildren are of a disabled person; if only the rest of the world were the same."

In response to my activities questionnaire, grandparents contributed nearly a thousand activities they love doing with their grandkids; many responses, of course, overlapped. After all, which grandparent *doesn't* love reading, coloring (included in "arts and crafts," below), and playing games with their grandchild? I've combined all the overlapping responses, broken down the list into indoor and outdoor activities, and included some unique "one-off" suggestions from grandparents.

Reflecting the differences in energy levels and physical abilities between parents and grandparents, the most common grandparent activities were gentle and calm but, as you'll see below, some grandparents were as ambitious in their activities as they were when they were younger with their own kids. Of course, the activities reflected the age of the respondents' grandchildren—"peek-a-boo" and "making funny faces" were not suggestions from grandparents of adolescents. ☺

Many grandparents reported going online to the tens of thousands of creative activity sites; you should do the same to dive deeper for specific ideas in each of these categories. To again use "arts and crafts" as an example, the number of artsy and crafty projects for kids online is staggering, enough to fill a lifetime of playdates with your grandchildren (or at least until you run out of construction paper and white school glue).

Here we go:

INDOORS: reading; arts and crafts; beading; cooking and baking; homemade desserts; board games, card games, and puzzles; jacks, dominoes, and pick-up sticks; video games; homemade playdough, oobleck, and slime; movie nights (and movie afternoons);

make ink stamps with slices of fruit; watch sports on TV; dolls and dollhouses; action figures; cars, trucks, and trains; building with Legos, wooden blocks, Tinkertoys, and Magna-Tiles; pillow forts and indoor "camping" in a tent; dress-up and pretend; singing and dancing; karaoke and air guitar; make ice cream sundaes and smoothies; waffles and pancakes; peek-a-boo (and *video* peek-a-boo!); make funny faces and wear funny hats; teasing and tickling; solve riddles and brainteasers; tell jokes; hide-and-seek; video chats; piggyback rides; setting the table; hallway bowling; balloon tap; ping pong, foosball, and air hockey; online apps for sharing screen experiences with grandchildren; float paper boats or water bottle boats in the tub; fly paper airplanes in the hallway; make a hideout or a pirate ship from an appliance box; holiday and Sabbath celebrations.

OUTDOORS: outings to the zoo, petting zoo, amusement park, arcade, bowling alley; shopping mall, museum, and aquarium; picnics and playgrounds; all sports; Frisbee; sidewalk chalk; hopscotch; "mother may I," "red light, green light," "ring-around-the-rosy," "London bridge"; water table; mini-golf; feeding ducks, geese, and pigeons; skipping stones; biking; pony rides; boat rides, rafting, kayaking, paddle-boarding; swimming; easy hikes and nature walks; collecting pretty rocks and sticks, smelling the flowers and trees; backyard scavenger hunt; ice cream store and diner; bird and duck watching; build, paint, and hang bird feeders; hunt for insects with a magnifying glass; collect fireflies in a jar (and then release); fishing; a day at the beach, collect seashells, and build sandcastles; live concerts in the park; car-and-truck-spotting (firetrucks!); blowing soap bubbles; sledding, skiing, snowball fights; drive in the country.

SUGGESTED ONLY ONCE, BUT NOTABLE: apple and pumpkin picking; visit school on "grandpals day"; make edible sculptures of characters and objects with food (e.g. banana slices on skewers to make snowmen; butterflies made of pretzel twists and peanut butter; the hungry caterpillar made with marshmallows); asking grandkids to teach grandparents new skills and games; empty the fridge and play "grocery store"; giving each other mani-pedis; tie-dye T-shirts; taking virtual trips on Google Maps; mailing little surprises to grandkids; sharing lollipops; building "Rube Goldberg" creations and "marble runs"; mark their heights on the door frame; launch rockets; tea parties and picnics with stuffed animals and dolls; playing with Mommy or Daddy's toys from when they were little; science experiments; a tablecloth over the kitchen table to make a secret reading tent underneath (flashlight required); build a tepee with old sheets; build a house of playing cards; reading with the Moonlite storybook projector (remember the "View Master"? this is so much cooler!); puppet show with socks or paper bags; dance with your shadows; paint rocks; make a sundial; make a ball pit in an inflatable pool; family music band with instruments made from household items; write secret messages with invisible ink; do an egg drop experiment; grow magic crystals.

ARCHIVIST AND HISTORIAN

There's one very important activity for grandparents not listed above. You are the keeper of the family history for your grandkids. Parents with young kids barely have time to go to the bathroom, much less teach their kids about the family's legacy. So that's your job. Draw a family tree with your grandkids, scour old picture albums and scrapbooks, and teach your grandkids where they came from and who in their past made it possible to be where they are today.

Everyone reading this book has ancestors from the "old country," wherever that might be and however long ago it might have been. The story of how those ancestors arrived and how your grandkids came to be as a result is an important story for them to hear. And you might explain to them that you are also a grandchild; tell them what you know and remember about your grandparents. If not you, who will do this for your grandkids, and how will they know how lucky they are?

Consider keeping a journal or scrapbook of your grandkids' lives. Record their milestones, the funny things they said, the friends they made. Save souvenirs of your adventures with them to show them when they're older. Make new entries on each birthday—or after each visit. Your adult children may be journaling already (see "Your Legacy" in Part 1), but as grandparents, you have unique insights and perspectives about your grandkids which, if written down, will someday become a treasured memory book and meaningful family keepsake. At our daughter's wedding, her brothers read entries from their late grandmother's journal about their sister. It was almost like having her grandmother at her wedding, and it brought us all to tears.

Whatever activities you choose for your time with your grandchildren, never forget that your presence with them is more important than any and all activities. Just as when you were parenting young kids, you are your grandkids' idols, inspirations, entertainers, and role models. And how blessed you are!

Epilogue—
My Favorite Letter

Of the nearly 2,000 letters and emails I have received (www.HarleyRotbart.com) from parents in the ten years since the first edition of *No Regrets Parenting* was published, one stands out as being so "on point" as to making me want to share it whenever I can. It's from Stephanie Shestakow, now the mom of two under the age of five and a community college Art History professor. When she wrote this letter back in 2017, her first child had just been born. I think you'll see why I love this note (reprinted here with her permission):

"Thank you for your book, No Regrets Parenting. *I have a new baby and I'm already reading your work, trying to lay the foundations for time well spent with my son. I'm already putting into practice my own methods for making the most of my time with my baby. When he was first born, I'd sit him in his bouncy chair and go about my business—making dinner, making his bottles, washing dishes, etc. I'd turn my back to him, obsessed with an endless 'to do' list. He was also born this past December, so I had cards to write, presents to wrap, baking to do, the usual holiday activities. Once I received your book, I thought, WAIT A MINUTE. I can be making special memories with my baby just by including him in my daily tasks (in addition to special activities with him such as stories, playtime, etc.). So I moved that bouncy seat right next to me as I did dishes, showing him the different utensils, how to turn on water, how I wash, dry, and put away. I make his bottles and show them to him, put his hands around them to pretend to 'shake' the formula. I show him*

the food I buy at the store as I put it away, moving his hands to feel texture, showing him color, maybe even putting some things under his nose! Of course, this is all a lot of work. It would be easier to sit him down in his chair, or put him in his crib, and go about my tasks. As I've read in your book, it's okay to occupy kids to 'pull the house together' or get other things done; sometimes we parents have to. But your book caused me to switch my thinking from 'he's just a baby' like there wasn't much I could do with him, and now I involve him in everything. There are so many ways to make memories with a baby in the everyday things. It takes more effort but it's worth it. The day feels much fuller and richer and doesn't go as fast. He's only three-and-a-half months old but already I'm worried the time will go quickly."

And that's what I'm talkin' about, Stephanie! It's never too early to start . . . and it's never too late.

*D*r. Harley Rotbart has been a nationally renowned pediatrician, parenting expert, infectious diseases specialist, speaker, and educator for nearly four decades. He is a professor and Vice Chair Emeritus of Pediatrics at the University of Colorado School of Medicine and Children's Hospital Colorado. He is the author of more than 175 medical and scientific publications, and five previous books for general audiences: *No Regrets Living; Miracles We Have Seen; 940 Saturdays; Germ Proof Your Kids; and, The On Deck Circle of Life*, which was endorsed by baseball Hall of Famer Cal Ripken, Jr. Dr. Rotbart was named to *Best Doctors in America* for 18 consecutive years, as well as receiving numerous other national and local awards for research, teaching, and clinical work. He served on the advisory boards of *Parents* magazine, *Parents.com*, and *Children's Health Magazine*, and has been a regular contributor to *Parents* magazine. "Coach Harley" coached youth baseball and basketball for 16 years, including eight years at the high school level.

Dr. Rotbart and his wife, Sara, still practice *No Regrets Parenting* on their three adult kids and now practice *No Regrets* Grand*parenting* on their grandchildren.

Andrews McMeel Publishing
a division of Andrews McMeel Universal
1130 Walnut Street, Kansas City, Missouri 64106

www.andrewsmcmeel.com

21 22 23 24 25 VEP 10 9 8 7 6 5 4 3 2 1

ISBN: 978-1-5248-7057-7

Library of Congress Control Number: 2021941869

Editor: Samantha Jones
Designer: Sierra S. Stanton
Production Editor: Meg Daniels
Production Manager: Cliff Koehler

ATTENTION: SCHOOLS AND BUSINESSES
Andrews McMeel books are available at quantity discounts
with bulk purchase for educational, business, or sales promotional use.
For information, please e-mail the Andrews McMeel Publishing
Special Sales Department:specialsales@amuniversal.com.